A CIGAR IN BELGIUM

Journeys of a Narrowboat

A CIGAR IN BELGIUM

Journeys of a Narrowboat

ANNE HUSAR

Matador
9 Priory Business Park
Kibworth Beauchamp
Leicestershire LE8 0RX, UK
Tel: (+44) 116 279 2299
Fax: (+44) 116 279 2277
Email: books@troubador.co.uk
Web: www.troubador.co.uk/matador

ISBN 978 1783061 143

British Library Cataloguing in Publication Data.
A catalogue record for this book is available from the British Library.

Typeset in StempelGaramond Roman by Troubador Publishing Ltd

Matador is an imprint of Troubador Publishing Ltd

The events related in this book are true as far as my memory and diary can be relied upon. There will almost certainly be
mistakes and inaccuracies and for these I humbly apologise.

For Oliver and Amy

May they continue to be understanding. Thanks also to everyone who has helped and encouraged me to finish this book especially Terry and Carole, Val and Koos and of course Skipper without whom none of this would have been possible.

ACKNOWLEDGEMENT.

An abridged version of 'Stuck in Walloon' as recounted in Chapter 6 first appeared in Canalboat magazine.

CONTENTS.

LIST OF ILLUSTRATIONS.

INTRODUCTION.

If you can look into the seeds of time,
And say which grain will grow and which will not.

Willliam Shakespeare

It was getting more and more difficult to get the children to go to bed now that they were in their early teens but at last the oldest had stomped off upstairs where the youngest was already asleep and we could sit down and have a quiet chat. Very soon our conversation turned to the future as it often did at that time and what we may want to do with our lives when the children had finished in full time education and were less dependant. One word summed it up – travel – but beyond that we hadn't really thought. That year saw in a milestone birthday which just had to be celebrated in a special way. Into my head popped the idea of a surprise canal boat holiday and it wouldn't go away. Eventually I gave in to it and booked us a week's hire on a 45 ft narrowboat. That birthday treat would turn out to be the start of our future.

Over the following years we inflicted more hire boat holidays on our growing teenagers who quickly got bored with the slow pace of life on the canals. They couldn't understand that this was just the element that we were enjoying and it wasn't long before we were devouring the boaty magazines dreaming of our own narrowboat. The ideas pictured in these glossy mags led to many evenings spent designing an imagined narrowboat layout on long pieces of paper spread over the kitchen table. We were getting more and more enthusiastic but the whole idea was still only one of many possibilities, wasn't it? Who were we kidding? It was becoming increasingly difficult to think of anything else.

There were about 150 boat builders to choose from, a seemingly impossible task so we went to a few boat shows and asked some of the established boat traders and brokers there who they would use to build themselves a boat. The same four names kept cropping up. All of a sudden it was going to be easier than we had thought and less easy to find excuses not to go ahead. We found time to visit the four and made our choice, a boat builder based at Braunston, the village that was well known on the 'cut' (as the canals were called) as the historic centre of the canal system. He had a year long waiting list, disappointing but it would give us cooling off time.

As we waited for our turn on the boatbuilder's list our designs were drawn and re-drawn until we hoped we'd got it right. Talking to other boat owners the consensus of opinion was that it wasn't until you'd fitted out your third boat that this degree of complete satisfaction was achieved. We hoped they were winding us up and stuck with our plans but did wonder at this point about naming our boat *Never Again 1* and then got side-tracked and started thinking of actual names. *Dragon Fly* might be pretty and we stuck with this for quite a while until we saw there were already lots of other boats using it. Choosing the right name was almost as difficult as choosing the boat builder. It was in the pub one night that Skipper had his eureka moment, sketching some thoughts on a beer mat. If we could incorporate 'snail' into the name, we could paint Less Cargo Carrying Co. on the boat sides, both a pun and a nod towards the history of these boats. Okay, let's look up 'snail' in our wildlife books and see what we can come up with. All of them featured a common water snail called the wandering snail and what could better describe us? Another decision made and we both realised that we were most certainly not 'cooling off'.

We had decided that we wanted the boat builder to make us a 'sailaway'. This would simply consist of the boat shell with glazing in the portholes and side doors. The interior would be empty apart from the engine which the boat builder would fit for us in the stern of the boat. All the rest, the interior fit out, plumbing and electrics would be down to us or rather more accurately, Skipper. The major decision regarding the boat's length had already been made. As we hoped that this would eventually be our home we wanted as much room as possible so went for a 'full length' narrowboat, in other words 70 foot long. Now this might sound a lot and sat in our 45 foot wide house realising how much more it would extend outside was scary but the fact that it was only a smidge over 6 foot wide (the clue's in the name) meant that fitting everything in that we thought we would need was a big challenge.

The big day came at last when our boat was craned into the space prepared for it at the end of our garden. The village turned out to watch as our 22 tons of pride and joy swung over the hedgetops and landed, more or less, on the waiting railway sleepers set into the ground. We couldn't wait to get inside, it was all so exciting this dream come true and it was around this point that reality struck when we found ourselves standing in a very long and very empty tube. It was impossible to imagine this vast, bare space ever looking like the lovely narrowboat home that we had spent so long planning for, or perhaps that was why we were experiencing the sickening rise of panic, because we could now imagine the amount of work that would be needed. Heroically over the next two years Skipper spent every evening after work and every weekend making the miracle that would be our new home. He already had the cabinetmaking skills required and cleverly learnt the rest. Friends turned up willingly when asked and they also took photos for us to keep of the slowly evolving and very beautiful interior. And will we ever forget the painting party? One hundred and forty foot of boat is a lot to paint but again friends rallied round, encouraged by the offer of liquid refreshment and the chance to wear all white, baggy coveralls. On a gloriously sunny and happy day the undercoat went on, enough to protect the outside from the elements until we were ready to decide on the final livery, another tough but fun to make decision. All was so well with our world, our future was looking very bright.

Then out of the blue, Skipper became ill. Overnight our income was halved and by the time it had become apparent that he would probably never be able to work as a cabinetmaker again, our debts were mounting. We would have to sell the house and think again. It took a long while to sell, the bubble was beginning to burst in the property market and prices were falling. We had our nearly finished boat craned out and put in a marina in the Fens which were our nearest interconnecting waterways. By the time the house had finally sold the children were not children any more and had decided on their futures. All we had to do was make a decision on ours. It took three weeks to clear the house and our lives of all the extraneous stuff that had so easily accumulated over the years and we moved on board *Snail* with what was left.

THE BOAT.

It was against all the advice in the 'Boating in Europe' books we had so avidly read. They all baldly stated that a British narrowboat WAS NOT SUITABLE for the wide waterways of the mainland. Their reasons were varied but were all based on the belief that the length : width ratio would make the boat unstable. The wash from commercial shipping combined with wide, often windy waterways would just be too much for a narrowboat and the dire consequences of taking such a boat into these manifestly unsuitable conditions were left to our imagination. Researching any topic will yield results that are not palatable and endeavouring to keep our spirits up we also sought out books, articles and blogs of narrowboats that had dared to put their hulls into the waterways of mainland Europe and survived the experience. Reading these accounts, the massiveness of all aspects of the European network graphically became apparent. The width of the canals, the locks, the commercial barges, just about everything was huge. In England our 70 ft long narrowboat was one of the big boys on the 'cut'. In Europe it would be less than a twig floating along. Food for thought but not for giving up. A narrowboat it would be.

At this point I want to make it clear that now we have experienced boating in Belgium we can confidently state that probably any narrowboat would manage the waterways of Europe. The only other narrowboat we met in our first year of cruising in Belgium had no modifications at all and was in her ninth year of problem free European travel. If it's working well in England, it will very likely work well in Europe but as we did not yet have a boat we had the opportunity to build in a few modifications. With the smattering of knowledge we had gleaned from our reading it would have been absurd not to incorporate a few changes that might turn out to be useful. But it needs repeating, a well maintained narrowboat plucked from the Grand Union Canal and put straight in to the mighty Gent-

Terneuzen Canal would feel at home, even if the skipper did not. Simply because we could, what follows are the adaptations we asked our boatbuilder to incorporate for us.

Stability.
If stability really was an issue, we wanted to make our boat as stable as possible. This meant heavily ballasting but if we used a double layer of concrete slabs instead of a single one as is the norm, Skipper would have quickly developed 'dowager's hump' with the lack of headroom. To prevent this unfortunate deformity our boatbuilder made the base plate from 15mm. thick steel instead of the more usual 10mm. giving Skipper the opportunity to stand tall throughout the boat and weight where it was required. The boat has now been through some very choppy conditions in Belgium and we do pitch but rarely roll. Visitors onboard comment on how amazingly stable she is. Whether this is due to the build or as I prefer to think, most narrowboats are inherently stable, we will of course never know.

Overheating.
We had read letters in the British waterways magazines from narrowboaters who were experiencing engine overheating. The expert's answer usually pointed out that modern narrowboats were built for small canals where cruising long distances at high revs was unusual. When used for river cruising however the skin tanks were not always of a sufficient size to cope with the cooling demands of the hard-working engine. Belgium has not got any British sized canals. Skin tanks twice the normal size were built in and we've never yet overheated.

Tanks.
Staying with the subject of tanks the ones to hold water and diesel on our boat were constructed as capacious as space allowed as we were not at all sure how easy these essentials would be to find on the waterways of mainland Europe. We had also heard worrying reports of boats in Europe being boarded by officials and fined very heavily for allegedly using red diesel for propulsion and there is no provision there for the 'splitting' of tax on diesel as there is in the UK. Having decided on an all diesel boat two tanks were built, one for red diesel in the bow to use for heating and cooking and one for white diesel in

the stern to use for propulsion so there could be no grounds for prosecution.

Toilets.

Holding tanks for toilets are a very different matter. We knew that most European boats were equipped with sea toilets. These pump their contents straight into the water, be it inland or coastal. We also knew that the rules were a-changing and that this murky practice was becoming as illegal in the rest of Europe as it is already in Britain. However although that legislation is now in place, the sanitary and pump-out stations are not so boaters here simply continue as before. We had to think carefully about our choice of loo. We chose to 'compost'. Not without its problems although the new generation of separating, 12v toilets are a great improvement. At least we do not have a constipated boat, searching desperately for non-existent relief.

Engine and prop.

We continued to think 'big' when deciding on the engine and propeller size. The 'Boating in Europe' guides advise their (mainly) cruiser owner readers to have enough power in reserve to speed away from problems. What was good advice for them seemed sensible for us lesser mortals. Accordingly instead of the more normally fitted 45hp engine, our 65hp Perkins gives reassuringly more oomph when needed. In conjunction with finding out and then fitting the best size of propeller to get the most out of the engine we confidently manoeuvre around ferries, commercials, erratic cruisers and boy racers. Often our unexpected turn of speed tends to surprise.

Anchors.

Adequate anchors could be handy if all this bold propulsion unexpectedly dies, especially if negotiating a strong flowing river or tidal waterway at the time of its demise. We decided it would be prudent to have two, one each end of the boat. There's not much room at the stern end of a narrowboat to store a large anchor. Ours sits outside in a purpose made anchor- shaped recess set into the side of the boat awaiting events that we hope will never happen.

Bow thrusters.

Bow thrusters are regarded as silly toys by many seasoned narrowboaters in the UK and this aid to steering is indeed not necessary on narrow canals even on windy days. In Belgium however it does help you save face when commercials are waiting and waiting for you to join them in a lock (time's money) and your bow is responding rather more to the forces of nature on a wide waterway than to your efforts. Or if a jobsworth lockkeeper happily lets you rope up on one side of his lock then strides out of his office and demands you 'just' move over to the other side instead, no reason. And always with an audience of other boaters...

Bollards.

Locks are just as enormous as the books say with each year new ones being built ever bigger to accommodate even bigger ships. There is absolutely nothing on the British canal network that can prepare you for the extreme pull on the ropes you will experience in a commercial lock when the shipping you will share it with enters or leaves, something we were made uncomfortably aware of very quickly when we came to Europe. To be able to safely rope up and keep anxiety levels down, extra bollards welded or bolted to the gunwales that you can put a turn of the rope round to help take the strain of a fast filling lock or whirring commercial propeller is one addition I really would recommend.

Preparing for Go.

Reading all the advice on how to comply with the myriad of rules and regulations that our length of boat appeared to have to meet could easily have panicked us. How could we possibly prepare our narrowboat so that it was safe, sensible and did not keep attracting the unwelcome attentions of the water police? The books implied that because our boat was so long (breadth never seems to be considered) we would have commercial regulations applied to us. These would be near enough impossible to inflict in their entirety on our poor little boat let alone the expense. We stopped reading, crossed our fingers rather irresponsibly and did what we thought would be enough. So far on our travels this has proven to be ample preparation but when bringing your own boat over feel confident to ignore / incorporate / improve on what follows.

Masts.

It has to be said that masts look faintly ridiculous on a narrowboat and we have two so doubly so but they are useful additions for all sorts of reasons. They keep lights and radar reflector at a height that a commercial just might be able to see us when coming around that blind bend. We have since been told by a commercial skipper that the radar reflector is a waste of space because at 2.5m above the waterline it is not high enough to be picked up. We keep it on though, just in case he's wrong. The mast lights that we hoped would be an adequate response to the requirements of the regulations consist of front and rear facing white lights and an anchor light. The latter is light sensitive and comes on automatically which is very useful for peace of mind on our black boat if moored overnight on a canal or river that has commercial traffic moving on it all hours. While on the subject of lights, our navigation lights are mounted each side of the boat in red and green wooden surrounds. They are bigger than those normally found on a narrowboat but not as big as the regulations seemed to suggest we needed. These would have put the boat in danger of sinking under their weight. The masts are also ideal for aerials. Our fixed VHF radio, FM and local TV aerials are all accommodated. Masts are also just right for attaching flags. On leaving England we began with just one, the small 'courtesy' flag of the country we were cruising. As we visited harbours and festivals we were enthusiastically given many more as souvenirs. We now have enough to ring the changes and they look colourful and fun fluttering in the breeze as we go along, reminding us of the friendliness we frequently encounter.

VHF radio.

Recently Belgium alone decided that all boats using their waterways should have two VHF radios or 'mariphone' as it is called. We already had a hand-held radio which had been perfectly adequate for calling up lock and bridge keepers. It was also useful for listening in to the chat between commercial skippers, not that we can understand their Flemish dialects but simply as an early warning that they are around and must be fairly close if the hand-held is picking them up. This can be useful knowledge on bendy waterways. As this one VHF radio was working totally adequately for us we may have ignored this latest dictum. We decided however to comply and bought a fixed radio too.

We use them in conjunction as often it is helpful to listen in to two frequencies at once (although just one radio set on 'scan' also achieves this) and the portability of the hand-held is also convenient as we can take it with us when using our tender. We have since heard that this requirement has now been rescinded.

Tender.
Perhaps one of the most useful additions in this list of preparations was the inclusion on board of the tender. We opted for an American made all plastic folding boat we affectionately named *Origami* which we keep in a purpose made box on the roof. Its outboard motor is stored in the bow. The regulations for its use in Belgium include the carrying of a VHF radio (see above) and an all round white light but no extra licence is required if you have already bought one for your 'main' boat. Unlike on the UK's narrow canals the towing of a tender behind a long boat is easy here whenever and wherever we decide to do it. The locks are enormous as are the waterways so it never has to be separated although occasionally it is put alongside in a busy lock. It is used whenever we want to visit smaller and often disused waterways where our narrowboat can not go. It is also an effective way to discover the small canals that run through many of the cities and towns. Often the lift bridges in the centre of a town do not lift anymore but this is no problem with a dinghy. To be able to explore these little-used intimate canals many of which are medieval in origin, is exciting and revealing. *Origami* also helps us extend our mooring options. With her to get us to dry land we can moor the narrowboat on 'dolphins' (substantial metal posts set into the river bed) well away from the bank or even if we're feeling adventurous simply put out an anchor.

Ropes and pins.
Mooring pins are of little use in Belgium. There are very, very few canals that do not have commercial traffic on them and the pull created by the first of those to go by however considerately will pull out the stoutest, strongest, longest mooring pin. We always rope to the bollards or rings provided and are glad we decided to upgrade our ropes to a thicker diameter than would be necessary in Britain. Centre ropes are useful too and are often utilised as 'springs' which can make the difference between a good night's sleep or a very

uncomfortable one. In addition to the 10m length ropes we usually use we also included twenty metre long ropes available bow and stern for locks where the rope attachment points are shall we say, limited. This is also when our improvised 'hook on the end of a pole' has proved invaluable as an aid to get the rope around that just out of reach bollard.

Fenders.
Adequate fendering in this unforgiving environment means off with the attractive but useless traditional small rope fenders that were all we needed on the UK system and on with the long, rubber 'Z' fenders the commercials use. Tyre fenders are only allowed on tugs in Europe and must never be used in a lock unless you want to see how irate a lockkeeper can become. We have however several ready for use when moored up. They are easily adaptable for the diverse moorings that a narrowboat has to cope with. We use them singly or roped together to absorb the impact of the considerable wash from passing vessels. An assortment of inflatable fenders would also do the same job.

Gangplanks.
A gangplank and a ladder are very useful. Ours is a 'two-in-one' three metre long aluminium arrangement. Yet more clutter on the roof but invaluable for climbing up a high wall that can sometimes be the only mooring available.

Roof space.
The roof of our narrowboat is thoroughly utilised for extra storage space. Here alongside purpose built storage boxes you will find the time-honoured paraphernalia of the live-aboard narrowboater. Bicycles and jerry cans mingle with boat hooks and pots of herbs, a touch of England on Belgian waters. Jerry cans are useful when the nearest shops are several kilometres away or a garage close to the waterway is offering white diesel at a price you can't ignore. Our roof also supports a canopy over the steering end of the boat fondly known as the 'carbuncle'. It's another addition that doesn't improve the look of the narrowboat but does add to the well-being of skipper and crew when cruising in all weathers. It keeps us and the dog dry and warm with the sides down when the weather is reminding us of

England or protects from sunstroke (yes it can get that hot in Belgium) with the sides up.

Miscellaneous additions.
These include a flag pole on the tiller for the Red Ensign, life rings and a rope ladder fore and aft as unlike UK canals you can't stand up in these ones if you fall in; binoculars to give a bit of advance notice of what's going on at a lock; spares for engine, pumps, etc – as many as you can carry as parts are much more expensive here and often difficult to source; a mosquito net that totally encloses the bed to keep the little blighters out from April to November.

Canine and human preparations.
With the boat now bristling with goodies, what about us? And the dog. These preparations involved some forward planning. Our passports still had several years to run as did our EU Health Insurance cards but dog passport arrangements (for bringing him back again to the UK) needed to be commenced six months beforehand and involved several visits to the dreaded v.e.t. These regulations have since been made easier so check on the Defra website for up-to-date requirements. Frequent foreign bank withdrawals were made less painful by opening a new account with a building society that (at the time!) did not charge for European transactions and also had the ever useful internet banking option available. In the months leading up to the 'off' we had both attended courses to gain the International Certificate of Competence including the CEVNI requirements and the VHF Radio Operator's Licence. These certificates along with the boat's newly acquired Small Ship's Registration document were put in a file that we keep just for boaty things. Boat insurance, diesel receipts and VAT invoices for the boat build are also there, an easy to find all-in-one collection to present to officialdom if asked. Our linguistic abilities have never been as good as the dog's who seems to be able to communicate whatever the language. A smattering of French and even less Dutch was supplemented by a couple of dictionaries and an optimistic outlook that we would absorb a useful vocabulary as we were exposed to it. We were now ready to go.

WHY BELGIUM?

This book is the first of two describing magical months spent aboard our narrowboat *Wandering Snail* in mainland Europe, Belgium to be precise. Please stifle the yawn, Belgium is not boring although I have to reluctantly admit that this cliché may have had something to do with our initial determination to commence our boating adventure in the Netherlands. Accordingly, when our boat was lifted out of an English canal and put back into the water at Terneuzen, a town in the Netherlands, we bought all the Dutch waterways maps while we were there and began to plan our route. Belgium's waterways, which we regarded simply as a through route to the French ones, could wait. It was a bureaucratic hold up in England unexpectedly keeping us waiting for post to arrive in Terneuzen on the Netherlands/Belgian border that led to our serendipitous change of plans. This enforced delay gave those hospitable and generous Belgian boaters who were at the same boatyard time to work their magic on us. When one of them eventually suggested (well insisted really) that we follow him and his boat to a market town in northern Belgium on an obscure river that we'd never heard of, we surrendered without hesitation. And so began our love affair with this unassuming little (it's the same size as East Anglia) country. Let's dispel some myths.

We've spent many years in Norfolk so we're used to the commonly held assumptions about its supposed flatness. The Belgians have to put up with this too. Yes, much of northern Flanders might not look out of place in the Fens where it is perhaps better to appreciate the skyscape rather than the landscape but go just a little further south and you have the rolling countryside of the Flemish Ardennes. If the landscape isn't to your taste, the Flemish architecture may well be. It can be breathtaking in all its gothic and baroque beauty and there's so much of it left to admire, even if some of it turns out to be modern replica following the devastation and occupation in the last two wars.

And then there's the far from boring Flemings themselves, almost unfailingly generous and friendly. From their embarrassing fluency with your language (it is not unusual for the Flemings to attend evening classes six months before a holiday abroad so that they can have a go at conversation) to their willingness to help in any way, they are a breath of fresh air. Their laid back attitude to all that life might throw at them is highly infectious as is the relaxed and always unthreatening café culture which graces every town and city. So many beers to sample but no drunken, troublesome behaviour and Belgium is certainly not the place to find employment as a bouncer, they are unheard of.

It is Walloon, that strangely named region of southern Belgium that has the scenery. From rolling hills to soaring rocky outcrops and dense forest, it is a delight to boat through. The Walloons are a little more reserved, rather in the French style and are less confident to try out their language skills but once through the initial reluctance, they too are equally generous and hospitable.

Because most pleasure boaters continue to regard the Belgian waterways as simply a quick through route to France, the best aspect of all for us is the relative peacefulness and emptiness of the system. Cruising for days in the height of summer and rarely seeing another pleasure boat on the move is just wonderful after the crowded experience that the UK canals often offer. But shh, we don't want everyone to find out that Belgium is a great place to be. This is our secret.

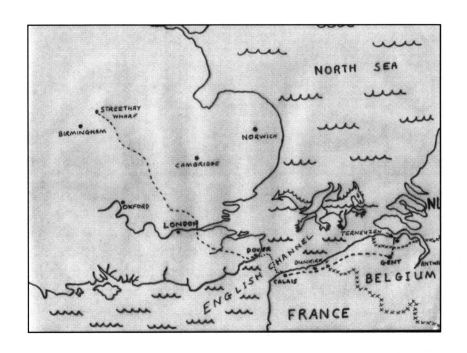

Wandering Snail's route from England to The Netherlands.

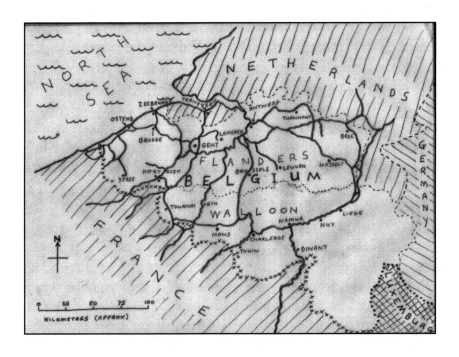

The Belgian Waterways.

CHAPTER 1.

Across the Channel – where *Snail* becomes less waterborne.

It was April 2008 and after many months of planning and dreaming, here we were moored at Streethay Wharf in Staffordshire in our narrowboat *Wandering Snail* with a hazy idea of a date to leave England sometime in May, heading for Holland. Sadly, leaving in our narrowboat was not quite accurate. That idea had been regretfully discounted when it became apparent that we would not be able to get insurance cover to cross the Channel under our own steam, even though a pilot and safety boat had been arranged and all the myriad of sea – going regulations complied with in a narrowboaty kind of way. We would have followed in the illustrious footsteps of Chris Coburn, Nick Sanders, Terry Darlington and the many others who had crossed the Channel braving this busy waterway in their narrowboats before us. But for us it was not going to happen. The many insurance companies I approached could not tell me why they had recently made this blanket decision. They all agreed there had not been any losses at sea but would not be moved. So there it was, either risk the crossing without insurance or go by road. We booked the lorry.

The boatyard at Streethay was a lively, friendly and thriving boatyard with a slightly chaotic ambience. It was run by the irrepressible Ray who with a twinkle in his eye, could never be persuaded to commit to a firm decision about anything. But we needed to know the date we would be leaving. When had he arranged the crane and lorry that would take us to Terneuzen, our chosen destination that was just over the border of Belgium and into Holland? There was so much to arrange before we left and we had an impossibly long list of things still to do…

While she waited, *Wandering Snail* was moored alongside an ancient, time-worn wooden and riveted iron ex-working narrowboat that was awaiting the attentions of the skilled team at the boatyard. It was serenely beautiful and seemed to say, "This is what a narrowboat should look like" while looking down at us from its noble bow. Our new boat with its faintly ridiculous twin masts and other peculiar additions for European travel did look far removed from the original traditional design of these lovely, purposeful craft. We hoped that all our adaptations that we were hastily finishing would be enough to equip us for the very different conditions abroad but did not have any real idea. Eventually we could do no more and it was time to find out. Suddenly, unexpectedly, Ray gave us a date. We would be lifted out the following week, the first day of May.

The crane that had been hired to take *Wandering Snail* out of the water and onto the lorry trailer finally trundled into the boatyard at Streethay very late in the afternoon. Already the plans were in disarray. We were supposed to have been well on the way to Dover by now, not still afloat on an English canal. *Snail* was manoeuvred into place and the lifting straps were placed under her. The crane driver pulled the lever and with a sound of straining canvas and dripping water our boat finally left the familiar and comforting English canal system but at a heart-stopping nose down angle. Poor *Snail* was rapidly returned to the canal and the straps were realigned. It took three attempts before she was lifted at anything like a straight angle by which point we could no longer watch. It was an unexpectedly emotional moment. Seeing our home swaying gently and freely suddenly made real this decision we had taken. We were leaving the known for the unknown. England and all that was English would be replaced by mainland Europe and all that was Continental. There be dragons.

Using cryptic hand signals the crane and lorry drivers deftly swung *Snail* over the boatyard and onto the trailer with its cradles waiting to take her. By the time she was properly secured it was much too late to leave. There was nothing for it but to visit the pub for a last 'proper' pint, a bar meal and a perusal of the maps with boater friends and staff from Streethay. I don't think it had quite dawned on us at that point that we would have to spend the night in the boat on the lorry. Somehow we clambered up and in, picking our way through the jumble of cardboard boxes full of newspapered breakables that covered the floor of the boat. We hoped no-one was standing near the drain holes when we used the shower in the bathroom that was now ten feet above the ground.

Sid the driver and his son Ryan woke us with the sound of the lorry's engine starting up, keen to be off at 4am. Sleepily we slithered down the side of the boat, dog tucked under an arm and resumed our slumbers in the back of the cab. It was an uneventful ten hour journey by road and ferry through France and Belgium to Terneuzen, our eccentric cargo attracting open-mouthed stares wherever we stopped. The Dutch boatyard was welcoming and efficient and soon *Wandering Snail* was lifted off the trailer and lowered into the water. It had been a very long day and rather tedious, but at last we were here and our spirits soared. It was the beginning of an adventure.

Skipper was directed to the only mooring space still available. It looked impossibly difficult to manoeuvre our extravagantly long boat into. The audience of watching cruiser owners wordlessly conveying the terse message, "Do not touch my boat," helped concentration. This marina was full of well manicured yachts and expensive glittering white cruisers. *Snail* had never before moored with such sophisticated but short neighbours. Her stern projected so far on the unsuitable 'finger' pontoon that she blocked the waterway behind her. Nothing could get past, not a good beginning for fostering international relations. The audience melted away. Not a word had been said. We hoped we'd made the right decision to come to Europe. This watery world was already proving to be uncomfortably different. Wearily, we began to unpack.

Crossing the dual carriageway outside Streethay Wharf.

Nothing can get past.

Gent-Terneuzen to Lokeren.

CHAPTER 2.

Terneuzen to Lokeren – where *Snail* is embarrassed.

The rain that had helped to dampen our spirits on arrival yesterday stopped sometime in the night. We'd had so much sleep to catch up with that we hadn't noticed. We also hadn't noticed the sporadic rocking of the boat caused by commercial shipping creating waves when locking in and out of Terneuzen just around the corner from the boatyard. The dazzling, hot sunshine that greeted us when we opened the doors that first morning ushered in the start of a heat wave that continued for the next two weeks. We changed into summer clothes and finished the unpacking with a glass or two of celebratory champagne. It was then time to explore our surroundings away from this sheltered marina with its gently bobbing craft where nothing had prepared us for the sight that was to meet our eyes just around the corner.

The boatyard and marina were at the end of a small branch off the mighty Gent-Terneuzen Canal. After a short walk we were suddenly looking at our first European canal 'in the flesh'. Our mouths dropped open, even the dog stopped rushing around to look. Creating a wash of narrowboat threatening proportions, an enormous tug pushing six equally enormous coal-filled dumb barges in front of it was leaving the lock. He seemed to be in a hurry. Then we saw the rest of the ships that had shared the lock with him were intent on overtaking. And these commercials were even bigger. The rolling waves created by all this churning propeller action came up the bank to lick our feet. Dreams had brutally become reality, how on earth would *Snail* handle this? All those preparatory trips on the tidal rivers Trent, Thames and Ouse and even that little sea crossing on the Wash, calculating tides and sharing the waterways with the very few commercial barges worthy of the name still operating in the UK, counted for nothing. There the biggest vessel we had encountered was 350 tons. That coal-laden load was over 6000 tonnes. This was scary stuff indeed.

Coal barge leaving the lock in Terneuzen with the road lifted to let it through.

The race for a Terneuzen lock.

We continued our walk along banks filled with wild flowers and headed a little way further for the shores of the vast Westerschelde. Crossing this wide expanse of tidal estuary would be the most direct route to reach the network of Dutch canals that awaited us when it was time for *Snail* to leave Terneuzen. Our little terrier thought the Westerschelde beaches were heaven-sent and played happily. We gazed out to sea, looking for the markers and buoys that showed the safe channels through the sandbanks. It certainly looked do-able in a narrowboat and we wondered why earlier in the day the boatyard owner had so strongly advised us against the crossing. We turned to throw another seashell for Woody to chase into the calm water and at the same moment caught sight of a fully loaded container ship in the distance. Also approaching was a sailing yacht which, with its deep keel was keeping carefully to the marked channel. The water that until then had been gently lapping onto the sand began to form into tall waves, reaching ever higher up the beach as the container ship got closer and closer. We called Woody and retreated to a safer and higher place as we watched the ship, also keeping to the channel, pass by startlingly close to the beach. Presently the fully loaded ship caught up with the yacht who now had nowhere to go, the narrow channel being all but filled by the larger vessel who, it appeared, had not seen the smaller craft. Miraculously, the yacht did not run aground but was tossed mercilessly about in the wash from the container ship as it pushed past. That could have been *Snail*. It was time to re-think our plans.

As it turned out, we had plenty of time to re-think, courtesy of a tardy response from the Small Ships Registry in England who still had not forwarded our certificate from the UK to us at the boatyard. We were advised not to leave without it so there was nothing for it but to enjoy the sunshine and explore Terneuzen until it arrived. The walk into town took us past one of the three locks that takes vessels out of the Gent-Terneuzen Canal and on to the Westerschelde. The biggest of these three locks measures 290 m x 40 m, the smallest 'just' 277 m x 24 m. For comparison, a typical English lock measures 22 m x 2.13 m. All three had wide road bridges at each end, one or other of which was frequently out of use to vehicles such were the constant locking demands of the commercial shipping here, for this is the gateway to the North Sea. The entire road complete with streetlights pivots high into the air to enable ships to pass through into the lock, a surreal sight on the horizon at Terneuzen.

Remembering to look right and left twice when crossing the road – this is the bike friendly Netherlands where cyclists have their own 'road' running alongside the usual one – we reached the town and its Grote Markt, the market place. This open space, often boasting a flamboyant town hall in the gothic style is a feature that is found in all towns both in the Netherlands and in Belgium. That day in Terneuzen we discovered a colourful folk festival in full swing, the first of many festivals we would stumble upon serendipitously on our travels that year. Sitting with a glass of ice cold beer at the table of a pavement café, soaking up the atmosphere, we knew then that we were going to enjoy European boating.

We were to be two weeks in Terneuzen waiting for the post. In that time we experienced many kindnesses and made new friendships. One afternoon returning from the beach, we found a box of cakes had been left in *Snail's* bow, a gift from the owner of the large cruiser moored next to us. The next evening we were invited on board for drinks and the skipper related the poignant story of his boat purchase. He had sailed the cruiser all the way from Malaga where he had bought it, back to Terneuzen where it had stayed ever since, this one cruise having been enough for his wife who decided there and then she'd had enough of boating. The following day a Belgian couple with a splendid yacht moored three boats away from *Snail* very kindly offered to take us shopping in their car and also generously volunteered to be a contact in case of emergency or any other need when we did finally get away. Over drinks on their deck one balmy evening they suggested we tried a Belgian cruise first to give us experience on quieter waterways before we attempted the much busier Dutch ones. They gave us a set of useful if a tad elderly Belgian waterway maps to encourage us with that thought and plied us with the locally made cold, smooth tasting and very alcoholic jenever as we discussed the possibilities. So it was that Ann-Marie and Guy were in a large part responsible for what turned out to be a lengthy and delightful journey around Belgium with its welcoming and hospitable people.

On our thirteenth day in Terneuzen, a small traditionally styled Dutch-built sailing boat arrived and moored nearby. It was lovingly maintained in all its beautiful detail by its Belgian owner Fernand. He was as interested in our boat as we were in his and another friendship was born. Fernand had a suggestion. The next day he would be cruising to the Belgian market town of Lokeren. Why didn't we follow him, moor in Lokeren for a while and he would drive us back in his car to Terneuzen to pick up the long awaited Small Ships Registration certificate when it arrived. Having several days before exhausted the delights of Terneuzen and anxious now to begin our travels, we accepted his very kind proposal gratefully. At last we would be on our way and even better, would have an experienced guide to hold our hand on the Gent-Terneuzen Canal, the only way out of here now that we had discounted the even more alarming Westerschelde option. Bright and thankfully not too early the next day, we cast off and followed Fernand's little boat up the arm and onto the Gent-Terneuzen keeping a sharp lookout for the 'big stuff' when we reached the junction. It was reassuringly quiet for us novices with possibly a commercial ship emerging from behind in the distance that we didn't have to worry about just yet.

"Wow, Fernand can't half keep up a pace. What engine's he got in that boat?" Skipper wondered as he began to lose us. He was getting further and further ahead of us before we realised what was happening. It was not Fernand racing ahead, it was us who were involuntarily slowing down. *Snail* had at that most inopportune moment developed gearbox trouble. She could only manage a meagre 2knots and the commercials were approaching fast. The mariphone as they call the VHF radio here, crackled into life with an impatient sounding Fernand. "Is that as fast as you can go? We'll never reach Lokeren today at this rate, please try to keep up!" Our boat name had never seemed so appropriate as we explained the problem. With enviable manoeuvrability Fernand quickly turned his boat around and took our proffered rope to tow us. We were so embarrassed and not a little anxious as commercials sped past with no consideration for our predicament. Heroically the little sailing boat took to its new role of tug with barely a shrug of the shoulders. Slowly, steadily, we were hauled through the choppy waters of this great canal and at last reached the junction with the Moervaart, the ancient man-made waterway that would take us to Lokeren. This first leg of the journey should have taken just two hours. Even with Fernand's best efforts, it had taken double that. We had missed our appointment with the bridge keepers who would take us through the lift bridges on the Moervaart so there was nothing for it but moor up for the rest of the day and wait for the mechanic to arrive whom Fernand had contacted on our behalf.

Another day, another tow. Patrick the mechanic had arrived the previous evening and had suspected gearbox failure but would meet us in Lokeren to make a further diagnosis. Looking resigned to his lot, Fernand made ready to tow us again, this time through the seven lift bridges along the route. After that he would leave us to crawl under our own steam, what was left of it, for the last stretch before the town of Lokeren while he went ahead. Unlike in England where boaters are so used to operating every feature on the waterway themselves, here in Belgium all locks, lift and swing bridges are done

Towed by Fernand on the mighty Gent-Terneuzen Canal.

for you by waterways staff contactable either by mobile phone or VHF. On the Moervaart the team operates only at certain times during the day and Fernand was desperate not to miss his booking again. Thus it was that the next few kilometres to the first bridge was one of complete Skipper concentration as poor *Snail* was pulled this way and that through the tight bends of the narrow river that Fernand knew so well, Lokeren being his home mooring, but which were so totally unfamiliar to us.

Vaguely aware while staring fixedly ahead that our surroundings were becoming ever more rural, the first lift bridge ahead rose as if by magic on our approach. Fernand exchanged familiar greetings and a joke with the bridgekeepers Ludo and Luke, who laughed at our unlikely pairing as we went under the platform they had raised for us. Once we were safely through, they lowered the bridge and raced ahead along the towpath in their bright yellow van to meet us at the next. This was a busier road bridge and we had to endure the stares of a large group of incredulous locals who had gathered around the barrier to watch. This was not how we had imagined introducing proud *Snail* to the people of Belgium. Would we ever live it down? Ludo and Luke were already practising their English on us as we passed with sentences featuring 'snail' and 'slow'. Fernand looked grimly ahead and we resumed our concentration. After the last bridge was raised for us and we had gone sedately through, our rope was returned to us and a relieved looking Fernand made a quick escape.

The remainder of our trip to Lokeren was achieved in a dignified sluggishness. It was early evening by the time we reached the town and Fernand had long ago moored up and gone home. We were relieved to see there was still plenty of space for *Snail* on the long visitor pontoons provided by the town and Woody was equally relieved to see acres of parkland stretching out behind the mooring. It was all very pleasant and for the first time in two days, we began to unwind.

It's now a few years since we made that first trip and we have got to know the Moervaart with its twists and turns very well. Passers-by and homeowners along the banks often recognise us and wave cheerily. They seem to have forgotten our ignominious start. Ludo and Luke however still refer to us with cheeky grins as the 'slowboat'.

Liftbridge on the Moervaart with a sea tjalk in the foreground.

*Following the Gentse Barge through an old factory bridge
on the Moervaart.*

CHAPTER 3.

Lokeren – where we encounter Belgian friets, market days and
another festival.

It was a sunny Sunday this first day in the town of Lokeren and dog
walkers on the footpath dodging speeding Lycra-clad cyclists
enlivened the view from our portholes. We began to be aware that
we were causing a bit of a stir. People were stopping to stare at the
boat and then searching in their pockets for a mobile phone to take
pictures. A few were bold enough to walk down the ramp and onto
the pontoon for a closer look. There might be thousands of
narrowboats in England but here our 'smalboot' as we overheard it
called was a rarity indeed. Feeling uncomfortably like a peepshow
exhibit, I fixed a smile and got off the boat to take Woody for his
morning ramble. It was good to merge unnoticed with the other dog
owners of Lokeren but as I walked it began to dawn on me that such
was our boat's novelty value, the unasked for attention was probably
going to happen wherever we stopped in Belgium. We would just
have to get used to it.

We had moored in Lokeren late the evening before behind
Fernand's pretty Dutch boat. By the time Woody and I had returned
from a pleasant exploration of the parkland surrounding us, Skipper
had offered Fernand a hand getting the feisty little sailing boat ready
for its summer cruising and was already scrubbing the decks. It was
the least we could do and Fernand had quite a list of jobs to complete
before he left. Later in the day they were joined by Fernand's wife
Irene, their children and grandchildren, all willing to raise the mast,
tidy the sails and carry things on board ready for the six month trip.
The boat was filled with good humoured chaos and unsurprisingly,
Fernand didn't get to the end of his list that day.

We were beginning to discover that Belgium ticks to a more unhurried clock than England. Next day we heard our post had arrived at the Terneuzen boatyard but it would have to wait, Fernand had a boat to finish. Patrick the mechanic might come over or he might not. There was no rush, *Snail* could stay in Lokeren on the mooring for as long as it took. We weren't in a hurry to leave, were we? Stay for the market, the cafes, the festival. Enjoy, enjoy.

Fernand leaving us in Lokeren at the start of his summer cruise.

Wednesday arrived dry and warm. It was market day in Lokeren and so well supported that it seemed all the inhabitants of the town had the morning off to go. Pensioners and young mums, cigar-smoking men and colourfully dressed middle-aged women crowded the cobbled market place and side streets, stopping to chat and gossip while they queued at the more popular stalls. The carillon of bells in the church tower came alive as it did every Wednesday for the market, playing its complete repertoire of well-known tunes, but only we visitors seemed to notice it. For the regular market goers this was simply an accustomed background to the familiar din found in all markets. This Lokeren market was no shoddy trestle table affair, instead the stall-holders arrived in gleaming, expensive lorry and trailer combinations especially made to open out hydraulically into mobile shops. The marketplace itself was studded with permanent electric hook-up points that were well used every Wednesday by these state-of-the-art vehicles who spilled out from the crammed market square into the side streets, enveloping road signs with their canopied slide-outs. It was a feast for the senses of variety and colour, local and exotic, fashion and frumpish, home and hand-made, fresh and cooked, but not much that was cheap or a bargain. For that you needed the unsophisticated markets of the Netherlands, where trestle table stalls were still the norm as we were to find out the following year. Nevertheless, this first experience of a typical Flemish market introduced us to the sights and smells that remain evocative of the special atmosphere in this northern half of Belgium.

Patrick arrived to remove the gearbox at 8pm that evening. He had brought along his partner to make an evening of it and anxious that we were introduced to some typical Belgian delights, suggested a treat of friets and frikadellen, the very popular Belgian fast-food of chips and meatballs, from the stall in the town centre. This would then be followed by a beer or two in one of the many cafes that lined the square. With cheerful anticipation we walked the few yards from the boat to the now empty market place and waited our turn in the small and popular 'frietshuis', that we now realise are as typical of every town in Belgium as fish and chip shops are in England. I think we were expecting something reminiscent of fish and chips but with a tasty continental slant. The polystyrene tray handed to us filled with fast 'food' of floppy little stick-like chips and meat of ambiguous parentage, the whole totally smothered in curry flavoured and vividly yellow mayonnaise was sadly far removed. Concealing our disappointment, we pretended to eat heartily so as not to offend and looked forward to drowning the lot with some tasty Belgian beer. Two days later and our consciences were troubled further when Patrick and partner arrived again at the boat to fit our new gearbox. They had also brought us a basket of new laid eggs from their chickens, a box of Belgian chocolates and a big bottle of beer from their local brewery. Such generosity was to become a regular feature of our Belgian travels.

The moorings had remained quiet throughout the many days of our stay until the day before the Lokeren Parktheater festival when suddenly we were joined by three gleaming white cruisers who had come to enjoy this one day spectacular organised and funded by the local community and businesses. The park behind us was steadily being transformed by many willing volunteers in anticipation of the thousands of visitors that came every year to enjoy the entertainment. This we discovered was provided all over the park and town and was amazingly, totally free of charge. The Lokeren tourist office was giving out programmes and tried to translate for us the Flemish descriptions of the acts. Our programme soon contained intriguing additions such as 'The Goose Parade', 'Mad Folk Group', 'Giant Glock' and 'Rather Rude Clowns'.

Festival day dawned and the threat of rain showers did not deter the crowds or the acts. The climate in Belgium is very similar to that in the UK, just a little warmer. When it comes to the vagaries of the weather, the Belgians are rather similar to the English and simply try to ignore it when they want to have fun. It did make the high-wire act that was taking place in front of the school buildings more dangerous than it already was, the performers gliding effortlessly up and down what appeared to be slender and now very wet ribbons and the geese that had been mentioned in the programme were also not going to be put off by a little rain. With heads held snootily aloft, they were led in a line by a clown through the crowds, marching their little pink feet in time to a drum played by another clown bringing up the rear. Perhaps you had to be there but it was an hilarious sight. There were more bizarre spectacles to be discovered in the park in this very Belgian gala. Giant 'giraffes', their heads bobbing high above the crowds, wobbled precariously on their camouflaged stilt legs. Comic 'monsters' in wheeled cages of gigantic proportions were pulled around the park, 'frightening' the children and parents alike. Clowns, mime, acrobatics and puppetry were all added ingredients to this eccentric festive recipe. Music of all kinds was to be found everywhere from a madcap folk group to rather more staid jazz and often with the opportunity for audience participation. The stage containing giant percussion including the enormous glockenspiel mentioned in the programme was especially magnetic for children whose parents would, I suspect, have also enjoyed the therapeutic effects of joining in. That the whole good-humoured festival was provided for free remained a miracle to us. It was a tribute to all the Lokerenese who so clearly enjoyed the yearly organising and funding. Long may it continue.

We now had a functioning gearbox again. Reluctantly it was time to leave friendly, generous Lokeren and head for the famous city of Gent. We did not know it then as we cast off the ropes but we were to return to this pleasant town many times.

The marching geese at the Lokeren Parktheater.

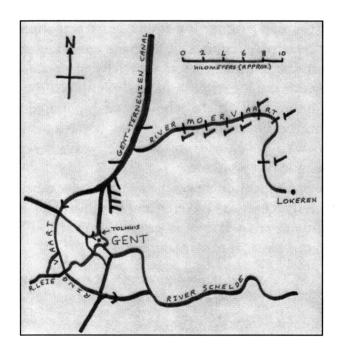

Lokeren to Gent.

CHAPTER 4.

Gent – where we get addicted to a strange alcoholic beverage and
meet an unlikely refuse disposal operative.

The morning of our departure from Lokeren was softly warm. I left
Skipper enjoying the sound of a happy engine with its new gear box
and took Woody for a last long walk along the banks of the disused
river on the other side of the town's bridges. Several years earlier
Lokeren had become the head of navigation on this river. Following
years of regular flooding the town had decided enough was enough
and had constructed a dam to control the water. There was no longer
any flooding for the town to endure but there was also no longer any
way through to Antwerp for boats. The wet-meadowland that
stretched along the banks where we walked was grazed by a herd of

Belgium's strangely muscular cattle, a type we would see often. With buttocks hugely out of proportion to the rest of their body, they looked as if they had enthusiastically followed a bizarre bodybuilding course. They lifted their heads to look as we passed, an incongruous sight amongst the dainty and colourful wild flowers all around them.

It was time to leave, the bridge keepers on the Moervaart would be waiting for us. Woody watched from his favourite viewpoint on the roof of the boat as we untied our ropes and pushed off. A few passers-by stopped to wave as *Snail* rounded the first bend in the river out of Lokeren and out of sight. I had walked this quiet stretch of river several times with Woody and it was full of wildlife. Quarrelsome ducks and chatty coots ganged up in the reed beds. Herons that hadn't quite got the confidence to stay put as we passed by squawking in annoyance as they flew off at the very last minute. A pair of kingfishers adding a flash of brilliant colour and enormous carp visible if you carefully crept up to them under a willow tree, sinuous in their spawning dance. I had also spotted a square, wooden platform on the top of a very tall post on the bank opposite and often stopped to watch a stork who was slowly and carefully renovating the remains of last year's nest high up on the top of the pole ready for the return of its mate. Magically this time as *Snail* approached two storks lifted their heads above the deep walls of their home to watch us go by.

In good time we reached the first lift bridge and waved cheerily to the waiting yellow van. Out stepped Ludo, grinning amiably, and put down the road barriers as a preliminary to lifting the little bridge. In England we would be doing this ourselves with the master key supplied with the boat licence. In Europe, this self-service is unheard of and is always met with incredulity when we explain the English way of doing things. Approximately halfway through the series of five hydraulic lift bridges on this river and we passed under a more primitive pulley operated structure that used to take lorries from the road on one side of the bank to a sugar factory on the other. This factory was now being demolished but next to it amongst the debris of twisted steel and concrete stood a solitary and ancient redbrick tower, a remnant of an earlier long gone manor house. On the top of the tower and turning in the wind was an ornamental golden dragon.

With its long, curly tail and gaping mouth it was an impressive and unusual weathervane. We took a photo and pushed on, anxious to keep up with that little yellow van, but already the germ of an idea was formulating in Skipper's creative brain cells. Perhaps *Snail* too could have a weathervane?After two hours following the twists and turns of the river Moervaart, the last bridge was operated for us and we pulled over to thank Ludo who proudly posed for us outside his surprisingly palatial new office while we took a picture.

Bridgekeeper on the Moervaart outside his palatial office.

It was now a short and straighter journey to the end of the river and the confluence with the Gent-Terneuzen Canal. Remembering *Snail's* antics the last time we were on this great waterway, it was with some trepidation we joined the 'big stuff', all en route to Gent. Thankfully this time our narrowboat ploughed effortlessly through the choppy wake left behind by the frequently overtaking ships and proved to be remarkably stable while doing so. We began to relax and take in the scenery. On both sides of this wide canal the industrial landscape stretched as far as the eye could see. There were factories and power stations all with active chimneys. At intervals the canal banks widened out to create docking areas where cranes were kept

22

busy swinging their metal jaws in and out of the deep holds of waiting cargo ships. The loads that we could see were varied and included gravel, coal and glittering mountains of crushed glass.

Up ahead, two tugs were slowly emerging from an arm of the canal and following meekly behind, a towering Tor Line ship was led out. It was so tall that it blocked out the sky as we passed. We learnt later that this enormous sea-going Swedish ship regularly used the Gent-Terneuzen canal to bring spare parts and completed vehicles for Volvo between Sweden and Belgium. We began to realise how important and well used these commercial waterways were in mainland Europe. They connected so many countries by boat using coastal and inland trade routes that were sadly no longer exploited in the UK.

At our turn off from this lively canal onto the arm that would take us to Gent itself, a noisy demolition site was hard at work. As befits a canal setting, the scrap metal that lay everywhere in tall, untidy heaps was all sourced from old and unwanted ships, their skeletal remains still clinging to the mooring bollards on the bankside. Awaiting her turn to be taken apart was an unexpected sight, the sad and rusting hulk of HMS Fearless of Falklands fame.

HMS Fearless waiting to be scrapped on the Gent-Terneuzen Canal.

Dodging one of the frequent and well used vehicle and bicycle ferryboats that intrepidly cross the canal from one bank to the other regardless of what might be in its path, we took the quiet turn-off to Gent and at 85m x 12m, our first European commercial sized lock. Here at the two storey lockkeeper's office we would buy our vignette, a boat licence which for the princely sum of one hundred euros entitled us to use all the Flemish waterways for a year. Unexpectedly it was also where we filled our water tank as it was here that we found out that many of the locks in Belgium have taps for bargees to use. Registration completed and with our new licence displayed on *Snail's* stern, the automated lock was quietly worked for us taking us by surprise and leaving our hosepipe dangling from the lock wall. These large locks or 'sluizen' as they are called in Flemish were really not too bad to manage after all with plenty of accessible securing points set into the lock wall for our narrowboat to use and a gentle ingress of water.

The mooring at Tolhuis.

Naively as it later turned out, our confidence grew quickly. The water in the lock reached a level, we retrieved our hosepipe and the tall, fern-encrusted lock gates swung open, revealing a wide junction with a variety of boats moored along the canal banks. Hopefully we could find a long enough space somewhere for *Snail* to join them and on the very end of a graffiti-covered wall opposite Tolhuis lock, where stone steps led up from the mooring quay to the road there was just enough room for us to squeeze in our 21 metres of boat. My first impression of our surroundings as I helped to rope up was of shabby apartment buildings and litter strewn grass verges. This was obviously not the upmarket end of town but with so many boats choosing to moor here it was presumably safe enough.

The couple on the smartly kept boat behind us had been taking pictures of our approach. They immediately introduced themselves as Anne and Hendrik and then invited us on board that evening for a drink with an opportunity for the skipper's wife to practise her English on us. It transpired that evening that Anne and Hendrik had already spotted us in Lokeren where they too kept their boat and would now love to show us the many Gentse delights, if that was okay? We could think of nothing better than to be guided around the city by this charming couple and arranged it for the next morning. It was a thirty minute walk into the historic part of Gent from the mooring or five minutes by the tram that grated noisily to a stop beside the bridge just ahead of *Snail*. Our guides thought it would be good to walk, we could go by tram another time. The walk took us through the Turkish quarter, full of colour and exotic smells. There were barber shops and cafes, all 'men only' with pungent cigar smoke wafting from each doorway. Jewellers' and clothes shops revealed a taste among this community for brightly patterned textiles and sparkling decoration. Anne paused to look at the fruit on offer at one of the many Turkish mini-supermarkets along the route. She suggested that we used these shops when we needed to stock up as not only were they the cheapest but also offered a good variety of meat, fruit and vegetables. We have since found this to be true wherever they can be found in Belgium.

The trams that had rattled along their tracks beside us veered off into the city as we came to an old bridge over one of the many intricate medieval waterways that wound through this ancient place. We had reached the oldest surviving part of Gent and the medieval buildings that surrounded us here were themselves surrounded by gaping tourists. We tried hard not to emulate them whilst taking in the elaborate gables and ornamental brickwork as we passed but it was difficult to remain impassive amongst all this gorgeous architecture.

Ancient house in Gent. Note the ship carved over the doorway.

Hendrik and Anne kept up a brisk pace as they were keen for us to reach the Vrijdag-markt, the historic and still functioning Friday Market place. This lovely market square was surrounded on all sides by yet more medieval Flemish buildings which were now used as very 21st century shops. Spotting that one of these sold electrical items, I mentioned to Hendrik that I was already missing BBC radio, especially Radio4 and would like to buy a Long Wave radio in the hope that this could be rectified. Now we were led to all the electrical shops within walking distance in Gent that Hendrik could think of and eventually his perseverance paid off. I was at last able to look forward to catching up with the Archers when we returned to the boat that evening. I hadn't realised that because our narrowboat was made of steel and consequently blocked the LW signal, the only way I could get any reception was to hang the radio outside the boat. Later in our travels the inevitable happened and a canal claimed my lovely radio. We are now on radio number two.

Anne and Hendrik were thorough guides and gave us enough knowledge that day to confidently explore the city on our own in future. By late in the afternoon it was time to walk back to the boats but we hadn't gone far before Hendrik stopped outside a dingy looking corner café. He was very keen to take us inside for another of Belgium's specialities. With memories of a previous disappointment concerning the 'friets' still clear in our minds but not wanting to appear ungrateful, we followed him into this unprepossessing establishment. The bar was dimly visible through the cigarette and cigar smoke. At that time there was no ban on smoking in Belgian's cafés which are similar to English pubs but do not serve food, you must visit a restaurant for that. Bottles of locally brewed beer on the shelves behind the barman mingled with little glass topped jars containing a yellow liquid and it was one of these that was put before me, along with a small cup of black coffee and a spoon. Lucky Skipper had got away with ordering a beer but what had I got to pretend to like now? I needn't have worried. This was home-made advocaat and nothing like the drink I remembered from my childhood. That idiosyncratic beverage from the 1950's containing a minute amount of advocaat was called a 'snowball'. It was made once a year in our house from lots of lemonade and just a little out of a bottle of runny, weakly flavoured, gaudily coloured goo. It was regarded as a special Christmas treat. The heavenly, creamily golden Belgian offering on the café table in front of me was similar in consistency to very thick 1950's custard but with the addition of an extremely alcoholic kick. I was hooked and this joyful combination of black coffee with a glass of Belgian advocaat, often with whipped cream on top as an added luxurious touch, is now an established late afternoon ritual onboard *Snail*. The beer was good too and the experience taught us to be confident in trying the cafés the locals enjoyed – this one was packed – rather than the more obviously touristy ones and not to be put off by appearances.

A traditional brown café in Gent, so called because of the heavy nicotine stains inside.

The next day our kind friends left in their boat for Lokeren and we were alone. Or so we thought. Just as we were getting ready to go back into Gent this time by tram, there was a knock on the side of the boat. Our first glimpse of Rik with his old clothes and wild hair made us wish we hadn't been so quick to open the door. Had we got any rubbish, he asked rather unexpectedly in hesitant English. If so, he would put it out with his. He knew it could sometimes be difficult on a boat to find a bin and he lived just over there. He pointed a finger vaguely in the direction of one of the scruffy apartment houses. Rather warily we gave him a full bag and watched from the safety of the boat as he made his way to the expensive looking Dutch-flagged yacht that had recently moored in front of us.

They didn't respond to his knock although we knew they were there and he shuffled off up the steps. This was bizarre, even for Belgium.

We made sure the boat was locked and set off to be tourists in Gent for the day. Here we enjoyed walks along the city's medieval waterways and panoramic views and another golden dragon weathervane from the top of the city's belfry. Finally we watched like delighted children as dark and white chocolate spewed deliciously from wide taps in an underground factory at a chocolatier's shop. We were beginning to like Gent a lot.

When we returned from the city Rik came down the steps to see us again, waving cheerily and introducing his wife Nelly. In flawless English she explained with a broad smile that they too were boaters but that their yacht was in dry dock a short walk away. Rik was fitting it out, hence the tramp-like appearance in his work clothes that morning. He had been on the way to his yacht when he had seen us moored below the wall and intrigued by our unusual boat, had made the excuse to knock. This was the start of an enduring friendship with this delightful, entertaining couple who in spite of many setbacks, remained inspiringly up-beat in their goal of sailing the seas with their beloved little red yacht.

Busy as they were during the day, Rik and Nelly devoted their time off in the evenings to show us the best cafés in town. Through them we discovered that Gent was a lively, colourful and totally unthreatening city even very late at night. We have never yet seen a 'bouncer' there and in fact had a problem trying to convey to Nelly what the word meant. Live music is still commonplace in the cafés of Gent and there are musicians enthusiastically playing to suit all tastes somewhere every night of the week, if you know where to look. Rik and Nelly were adamant that we returned for the Gentse Feesten, a twenty-four hour music festival held over ten days in July. It had been an annual event in Gent for one hundred and sixty five years so the organisers knew by now how to put on a good show and amazingly, it was all for free. We promised to come back.

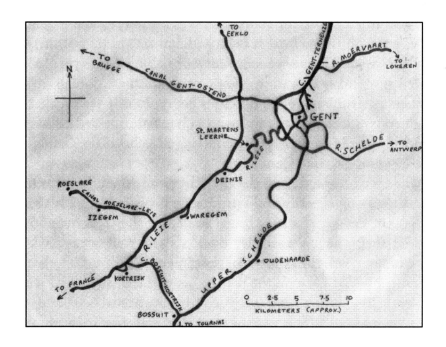

Gent to Kortrijk.

CHAPTER 5.

River Leie to Kortrijk – in which *Snail* knows her place, Skipper
develops his taste buds and we encounter Beguines.

The following morning Skipper returned from a Woody walk on the
edge of Gent full of news about an unusual commercial barge he had
encountered. It was a 'spits', the Belgian version of the French
peniche and at 350 tonnes now the baby of the commercial shipping
world. They were still a common enough sight on the waterways here
as the smaller French waterways network continued to provide them
with plenty of work. What was so unusual about *Floan* was her crew,
a couple of 60 somethings who both hailed from England where they

30

had worked a pair of narrowboats in the past. They had achieved their commercial skippers' licences twelve years or so before and had successfully made a good living with *Floan* on the European waterways ever since. As the conversation progressed, it became evident that another English owned and worked spits was also moored here in Gent, the *Pedro* and that as far as *Floan* knew, these two barges were the only ones to be operated by UK owners in the whole of Europe. Intrigued, we decided that we would try and find this other boat on our way to the River Leie out of Gent and as luck would have it, there she was waiting a load in Handelsdok just a little way from our Tolhuis mooring.

Roy and Carole with their pretty little Jack Russell saw us first and waved to us to come alongside. While the two dogs raced around *Pedro's* wide side decks, we learnt that they were in Gent waiting to be loaded with Canadian mustard seed. They would then make the twenty-one day non-stop trip to Dijon in France working on average a twelve hour day to deliver on time. Once there they would have a short breathing space to clean out the hold and stock up with provisions before taking on another load and returning to Belgium. This had been their way of life for many years and we total beginners in Europe mercilessly picked their very experienced brains for useful boating tips which they generously shared with us. Swapping email addresses and promising to keep in touch, we retrieved our now love-sick terrier and turned around to finally make our way out of Gent.

Our route took us along the Verbindingskanaal (it simply means 'connecting') where the eye-catching *Pussenboot* had its mooring. This colourful, converted spits housed stray cats and kittens all looking for new homes. Several of these waifs and strays were roaming about in an outside run and the sight of them got Woody so excited I had to prevent him falling off *Snail's* roof. Unperturbed by the fuss made by this silly little boat dog, their inquisitive gaze followed us as we passed by en route to the junction with the Ringvaart, a very wide and often busy commercial waterway which looped around the suburbs of Gent. This time however it was unusually quiet and we were overtaken by just one 1500 tonne cargo boat which created very little chop for *Snail* to deal with. Eventually we turned off this dull and monotonous canal onto the River Leie.

This waterway has a weight restriction of 100 tonnes so we expected a peaceful and very different trip. Scenic and very exclusive, this winding river reminded us of a narrower version of the Upper Thames except that apart from the occasional cruiser going past with their noses in the air, we had the river to ourselves. Stopping places were few and choked with small boats but it didn't matter, it was so very pleasant to just slowly keep meandering on in the warm sunshine.

Rolling countryside of fields and meadows could have become soporific but there were enough unexpectedly tight bends in this river to keep Skipper awake. Extra interest was provided by the many architect designed 'des res' houses lining the banks and looking down on we mere narrowboaters from large and impressive gardens that swept up from the water's edge. Amongst the manicured lawns and crisply shaped topiary there were some unexpectedly tasteless plastic garden ornaments adorning these palatial homes. On one lawn a herd of life-sized bright blue cows were arranged randomly and on another an enormous red bulldog glared at passing boaters. It was heartening to see the occupants of these riverside houses didn't take themselves too seriously. There were definitely no moorings to be had anywhere near these riverside properties with many 'privaat' notices pinned up to remind boaters of the fact and their place in the scheme of things and it wasn't long before our initial interest turned to resignation as these linear housing estates went on and on. The few public moorings provided were full already with sparkling white cruisers, their owners sitting on deck, glass in hand, often not even bothering to turn to look at poor *Snail* whose inferiority complex was growing by the minute.

It's always slightly worrying when evening has crept up on us exploring an unknown waterway and we still haven't found a mooring. This weight restricted and therefore quiet stretch of the River Leie would soon end at Deinze, a town at the junction with this river and a connecting waterway that linked it with the Gent-Oostendekanaal. This made the Leie accessible to commercial sized ships again so we were becoming more than a little desperate to find somewhere suitable to stop before we reached this point. Blink and you miss it, but just before the bridge and yacht-haven at St.Martens-Leerne I spotted a landing stage just long enough for *Snail* and, ignoring the trip boat signs nailed to the mooring, we were at last able to stop for what we hoped would be an undisturbed night. Very quickly the locals spotted us and crossed the bridge to say hello. Apparently the trip boat was not returning for a few weeks so we could stay as long as we liked. Having answered all the usual questions about the boat – why was it so narrow, what was it used for, how old was it (always an awkward question, do we lie or tell the truth and disappoint them?), they then told us about a good restaurant in the village, usually not encompassed within our monthly budget but tomorrow was my birthday. There was also a castle at the end of a good countryside ramble, all delights for the next day. The following afternoon, local recommendation duly followed and having enjoyed the walk, we sat outside in the sunshine with a beer or two on the converted barge that served as a clubhouse for the yacht haven across the river. Our reveries were interrupted when my mobile phone bleeped with a message from Anne and Hendrik, the boaters we had met in Gent. They wished me a happy birthday and added that they had found us a free mooring for the winter in Lokeren with water and electricity. What a present!

We moved on to Deinze the next day. The traffic was stopped and the town bridge lifted for us to pass under while we scanned the banks looking for a mooring. I needed some shopping and anyway this place looked worth a visit but the yacht haven was fenced in, locked and full and the banks of the river were lined with acutely sloping stone, all very uninviting. First however we needed to fill up with water. The bridge keeper had a tap for boaters to use set in the wall above an old and very rusty metal dinghy chained to the bank. To reach the tap meant a scramble over this leaky boat after we had tied up alongside it. We tried not to think of the scratches to *Snail's* paintwork which in spite of a judicious use of fenders were the inevitable consequence of this arrangement. Water tank eventually filled we moved *Snail* to the only possible mooring, the very narrowboat unfriendly sloping river wall.

Ignoring the grating sound from *Snail's* loudly complaining side as she scraped against the stones, Skipper got out the gangplank and I wobbled across, promising to shop as quickly as I could. Luckily there was a supermarket next to the bridge and with trolley filled, I joined the queue to pay. My turn at last, I handed over my Visa card and heard a collective gasp from the rest of the queue behind me. It was at this inopportune moment I learnt that much of Belgium did not accept 'plastic' payment for anything apart from with its own card system which is not accessible without a Belgian bank account. Newly arrived from the very card-friendly UK, this was a bit of a shock. With my trolley load of shopping in a heap at the end of the counter, the rest of the queue were desperately trying to convey to me where the nearest bank was that might swap Visa for cash. I ran out of the shop and across the bridge where, out of the corner of my eye I could see Skipper sun-bathing on the grass. This didn't help my mood although it was hardly his fault. I tried the cash machines of two different banks who both coughed out my card as if I was trying to poison them. Lucky third try and back I went to the shop, avoiding the faces of everyone stuck in the growing queue.

Back on board and it was obvious we would have to move on. This really was a totally unsuitable mooring for a narrowboat and probably for most other types of boat. Wondering why being on the river as it was, Deinze did not make their town more boat-friendly we pulled in the gangplank and carried on down the Leie, meeting several large commercials now that the river was wider. As a postscript, we re-visited four years later and Deinze had now indeed given their town quay newly constructed and inviting-looking moorings. Too inviting as they were so full of cruisers we could not try them out but they did look good. Just before we reached our second European lock near the town of Waregem there was what appeared to be a disused arm off the river. It looked very industrial on one side but rural on the other so we turned off the busy Leie to investigate and there at the very end were floating pontoons with lots of space to moor up. As we did so we wondered why the 'risers' holding the pontoons in place and that allow the mooring to go up and down with changing water levels were so unnecessarily substantial. The water was calm and the old lock and weir stream that we could see just beyond the mooring were apparently no longer used having been by-passed by the modern one that we had so nearly used back on the main river before we had spotted this arm.

The oppressive heat of the day was building into a storm as we took Woody for an exploratory walk, climbing up the hinged ramp at the end of the pontoon that led to the path along the water's edge. We soon walked the remainder of the arm and then joined the towpath along the main river where behind us we could see the massive new lock that had replaced the old one near our mooring. It was an interesting walk spent watching the varied types and sizes of commercial traffic going past the local yacht haven which was safely tucked in to the river banks. Here we noticed that *Snail* would have been too long to fit and were very pleased with ourselves that we had turned off onto the arm for the night instead. The wind was getting up and we headed for home before the storm broke. We noticed that the ramp back down to the pontoon was more level than it had been and *Snail* was rocking a little in the combined effect of a strengthening breeze but also in the slight current that was now being created by the old weir that had suddenly sprung into life. We stopped to talk to the crew of a cruiser which had moored in front of us while we had been walking. She was flying the Red Ensign and the couple on board turned out to know Belgium well as they often came over from England to spend time on their boat. We found it reassuring to hear that they regularly stopped on this pontoon and after a pleasant chat we returned to *Snail* to cook the evening meal.

The storm finally broke noisily overhead. Our terrified terrier unsuccessfully tried to ignore it by keeping busy snapping at flies. I discovered for the first time how useful the guardrail around the cooker was as it trapped sliding saucepans while we were fully occupied trying to keep our wine inside our glasses. Never had *Snail* been in such rough water but we knew the storm would pass and then all would be well. The rain continued long after the storm and its accompanying gale moved away. But why were we still rocking so violently? A quick look outside revealed the weir in full spate, the water rushing past the pontoon in wave after wave. We were in for a rough night which was not appreciated by Woody who could no longer distract himself and was promptly seasick. We discovered later that any risk of flooding in France is relieved by sluicing their extra rain water through Belgium, hence the overactive weir that night. And the need for robust pontoon risers.

This was the start of several days of rainy weather and next day the wild current produced by the still active weir made turning *Snail* around to return back up the arm and rejoin the river an interesting manoeuvre. We were bleary eyed and not too mentally alert after our bad night so breathed a sigh of relief when we reached Sint-Baafs-Vijve lock back on the Leie and found we were the only boat to go through. Neither of us were ready that morning to face the added anxiety of sharing a lock with the big stuff for the first time. Simply re-attaching the ropes to the bollards set in the walls as we gradually changed level was enough to concentrate on.

The mix of industrial and rural on opposing banks continued as we made our way to the Roeselare Canal junction where the meeting of canal and river is guarded by Ooigem lock. The greyness of the day did nothing to lift the drabness of the scenery as we tied up alongside a wall to wait for a commercial barge coming the other way that would be worked through the lock before us. We could see its bow towering above the lock gates as it entered the chamber and thankfully remembered to make sure *Snail's* ropes were tightly secured while we waited. It is impossible to manually hold onto them against the surge that these vessels produce as they gather speed when leaving a lock. Red light changed to green and we could at last enter the chamber. We were all alone in a lock that was 7.5metres deep, 12.5metres wide and 115metres long and looked like a little twig as we settled against the dank wall. Because it was such a long drop the bollards provided in this lock were 'floaters', that is they are placed in vertical channels up the walls and float up or down with the boat as the water level changes. We secured our ropes, gave a thumbs up to the lock keeper high above us in his tower and enjoyed the ease of managing in a lock that this method allows, the floating bollards doing the work for us.

The Roeselare canal is straight and bordered for much of its length by a railway, rather like many a British canal. The big difference in Belgium is that their canals are still heavily used for freight as well as pleasure. When we reached Roeselare town at the head of the waterway, cruisers had already filled the end wall and commercial barges lined the side quays. With no room for us we dispiritedly turned around and headed all the way back again. We were novices still. Later in our travels we would have the confidence to ask to come alongside a moored barge but this time the town of Roeselare remained unexplored as we made for a suitable wall we had already spotted when passing the town of Izegem on the canal earlier in the day. In its heyday, Izegem had been a famous shoe and brush making town. Now much of it was a building site as disused, redundant factories were being pulled down, the dust settling over *Snail's* paintwork where it was then glued on by the rain. Awoken bright and early the next day by the rhythmic racket of a pile driver we made the easy decision to skip the delights of Izegem and push on up the Leie again to the large and historic town of Kortrijk. It would mean negotiating two more locks but our confidence in our abilities had grown and we now felt much more experienced in what to expect. Of course we hadn't actually shared a lock with anything yet. This was about to change.

The rain continued as we got back to the junction and approached Ooigem lock. We called up the keeper on the VHF radio for instructions. The lock lights were on red and with no reply from the radio, we pulled up behind a waiting commercial barge hoping all would become obvious. In the fullness of time the lock gates opened and out came a spits, helpfully putting on much more power as he went past. We were to become very used to the resulting tidal wave but at that time in our travels it made anxious moments for we novices as the increased surge of water tugged hard at our ropes. This combined with the propeller of the barge in front beginning to churn as he pulled away to enter the lock and their breaking strain was tested to the limit. With still no response from the radio, Skipper decided to join in the advance, holding back near the lock gates while the barge in front roped up inside the chamber and then thankfully turning off his mighty propeller. It was a French flagged peniche and when they invited us to tie up alongside to them, we gratefully accepted. Secured to their barge it was very pleasant with this arrangement not to have to worry about adjusting our ropes as we changed levels in the lock and the young and friendly skipper's wife and I had time for a chat. While Woody who had been invited on board stretched his legs running around their enormous decks, I learnt that these pleasant bargees were on their way back to France where the River Leie would then be known as the Lys. Here they would pick up another load and return again to Deinze. The lock gates opened and although we were beckoned out first, the commercials that had shared the lock with us soon caught up and overtook. We returned a cheery wave from the French barge and continued on our way in our own time.

The river was becoming noticeably busier as we approached Kortrijk. We shared the next lock with the 'big stuff' and no problems although we were again ignored on the VHF. This being ignored was proving to be a slightly uncomfortable position to be in as we could never be sure when or even if to proceed. We have since tried a variety of polite verbal approaches not found in the VHF handbook to elicit a response from the control tower but rarely succeed and have come to the conclusion that being firmly at the bottom of the pecking order here, we are simply not worth bothering with. At last able to turn off the main river we moored on a visitor pontoon on the edge of the city of Kortrijk opposite a shiny modern hospital. Above the boat on the quay wall vehicles were parked frighteningly close. Ahead of us there was a car sized gap torn through the ancient railings that should have marked the edge and this had been temporarily filled with bright orange netting. On the opposite bank was a building site linked to a river widening scheme that had been visibly 'work in progress' all along the approach to Kortrijk. There would definitely be more dust on this mooring and maybe a car or two heading *Snail's* way too? Our reservations about mooring here close to historic Kortrijk were soon overcome by the free water and electricity that was provided by the city for visiting boaters while the works were in progress. This persuaded us to stay for a few days but mopping down *Snail's* sides became a twice daily ritual.

We eventually stayed in Kortrijk for six days. Every morning we would walk along the banks lining the waterway, over the twin towered packhorse bridge with its cobbled paving that was all that was left of the medieval defences and continued along the river to the alternative moorings that were provided at the other end of town. They were probably more peaceful than ours and were definitely more bosky but a low bridge at the junction with the Leie made them difficult to access without dropping *Snail's* masts. They were also very full with a variety of craft from the usual visiting cruisers

The twin medieval towers at Kortrijk.

through to large live aboard barges. One of the latter flew an English flag and we stopped to chat while Woody was indulged in his now customary game of running around the decks. We learnt that the cost of year round mooring here for their 24 metre boat was just one euro a day, a piece of information that we mentally filed away for possible future use and we were still chatting when Woody, deciding he had had enough came back up the gangplank. He flopped down next to us with a bored expression while we continued our conversation finding out what Kortrijk had to offer the visiting boater. As we talked, I became aware of a little man in a blue T-shirt with a large dog. For some reason he had stopped to stare at us giving the two dogs ample opportunity to get to know each other with much circling and wagging of tails. I eventually called Woody back and the man rattled off something in Flemish which didn't sound very friendly. It was then that I saw embroidered on his T-shirt the single word 'politie' which quite obviously in his case did not translate as 'polite'. He explained in Pink Panther Frenglish that it was the 'lur' to keep your dog on a lead at all times and this humourless individual was intent on us upholding the 'lur' while we were on his patch. It was suddenly evident who Peter Sellers had based his detective on.

Chastened, but with anarchy in our hearts, we carried on our walk to the historic part of Kortrijk. Here the streets were lined with perfectly restored buildings many of which accommodated beautiful shops full of expensive merchandise and the cobbled pavements were busy with chicly dressed Kortrijkians. Keeping our scruffy terrier on a tight lead, we window-shopped wide eyed like a pair of street urchins. Spotting an invitingly less pristine lime-washed archway set into an ancient high wall and looking incongruous amidst all this perfection we stepped inside and like Alice, into a different world. Narrow alleyways of crooked whitewashed cottages each with its own tiny front door all set among cobbled paths and herb gardens invited us to quietly explore. To speak out loud would have broken the charm of this tranquil place. The information boards placed unobtrusively around this medieval walled 'village within a town' told us a little of its ancient history. We had discovered our first Beguinage.

Centuries before, land had been given by wealthy citizens to be used by equally wealthy women who wanted a convent style contemplative life but with a 'get out' clause – they could leave to get married at any time. Known as Beguines, these women were often highly educated and founded many schools in which they also taught. Poorer women could apply to join the Beguinage too which gave them food and shelter for life in return for household chores. The Beguines were as self sufficient as possible, tending productive gardens and earning an income with their teaching and handicrafts. Outsiders were free to come and go through the archway that we had come through although it was and still is locked every night at 10pm. This way of life was a popular choice for many women who although pious, did not want to commit to the total discipline of a convent. Between the 15th and 17th centuries Beguinages were set up in several northern European towns and cities and thrived until surprisingly recently. The last Beguine died in the 1980's and those Beguinages that still survive are now protected as heritage sites, many with tenants living in them who carefully maintain and protect the special atmosphere that is found within the walls and which we so appreciated.

The Beguinage at Kortrijk.

Back at the boat the rain had stopped, the sun and with it the onlookers, had come out. I sat in the bow with a refreshing glass of kriek (Belgian fruit beer) and a book but reading became impossible as question followed question about our life and the boat. Resigned, I put my book back inside *Snail* and just as I did so there was a knock, knock on the porthole. On the pontoon stood two inquisitive men, trying to peer inside the boat.

"For goodness sake, let me at least get back outside." I thought grumpily and scowled at them through the open side hatch. I'd really had enough of this intrusion for one day and answered their many enquiries less than effusively. As they finally said goodbye I thought of a question to ask them. We had been looking for a shop that sold satellite dishes and the rest of the paraphernalia we would need to receive TV programmes (and I hoped, BBC radio – dangling the LW one outside in all weathers had long ago lost its charms) and had walked miles with no result. Did these two Kortrijkians know of a suitable shop hereabouts within walking distance? Francis and Ted shook their heads, "You need a car." they said, "We will take you."

It was a full two hours later that Skipper was returned to the boat with all three men carrying boxes of equipment. This kind father and son had driven to all the likely outlets on the industrial estates around Kortrijk until they had succeeded in finding everything that we would need. During the journey they had discovered Skipper's delight in all things brewed and Francis turned out to be a connoisseur of Belgian beers. He arranged to pick us up the next day and treat us to some of the contents of a café he knew. Now however they had to go as they were very late in visiting Francis' elderly mother in the hospital opposite which is where they had been heading when they first saw *Snail*. True to his word, Francis came back the next morning and gave us a lovely day out in the countryside around Kortrijk. Quietly spoken, generous and considerate, forming an instant rapport with Woody who adored him, he told us proudly of his family and of their links with England from the Second World War. His English was impeccable, invaluable not only for facilitating good conversation but also for translating the immense beer menu put before a bemused Skipper.

We have stayed in touch, often visiting Francis in his home or he finds us on *Snail* always with a gift of beers for Skipper to try. He looked after Woody for us when we returned to England one year on the motorbike and during that time taught him to "Leave those chickens!" which we have found also works for ducks, coots, geese… We feel very privileged to be able to call Francis a friend, especially after such an inauspicious start.

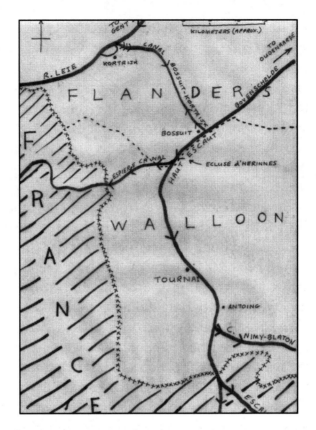

Kortrijk to Tournai.

CHAPTER 6.

Into Walloon to Tournai – in which Snail becomes Escargot, we lose some locks, get stuck in the mud and unexpectedly make music.

It was time to move on from Flanders and discover the other half of this sometimes uneasy Belgian marriage, the southern waterways of Walloon. We were not sorry to leave our sand blown mooring at Kortrijk. The canal widening works on the opposite bank were noisy and dirty with some amazing health and safety practices. The works supervisor, clipboard in hand, made a habit of teetering on the edge

43

of the crumbling river bank, hardhatless and lifejacketless as the excavator removed soil from around his feet. We would watch aghast, waiting for the splash.

We perused our second-hand Belgian waterways map that had been donated to us back in Terneuzen by Ann-Marie and Guy and found an invitingly small canal, the Bossuit, off the river Leie on the edge of Kortrijk. This rural canal had according to the map eight elderly, spits-sized locks for us to ascend. That was a lot of locks for such a short canal and they were all manually operated by a lockkeeper who used a bicycle to get from one to the other. Intrigued, we had walked with Woody the day before to the little office by the first of these locks and booked *Snail* for the passage through. We had hoped we would be able to save face by at least keeping up between the locks with a locky on a push-bike but unfortunately he turned out to be a fast worker. Not only did he seem to take great delight in racing ahead to have the gates open for us so quickly that he had time for a cuppa before we reached him, but once we were in each lock he also enjoyed racking open the paddles so fast that poor *Snail* strained uncomfortably on her ropes against the spectacular rush of water. There are times when I long to be wielding the windlass again. We survived locks one, two and three but then inexplicably travelled for a longer stretch than was shown on our map between locks three and four. We were also slightly concerned that we hadn't seen our speedy lockkeeper go past us on the towpath. As the next lock came into view we could see why. Totally unexpectedly, lock number four was large and modern. It came complete with a high control tower and was very, very deep. We roped up to the floating bollards inside the chamber and wondered what to expect next. Locks five and six turned out to be modern and deep too. We were now going back down rapidly and nothing like what we had been led to expect on the map. When the massive gates of lock six opened after we had dropped another nine metres or so, we made to leave for what we thought would be the penultimate lock of the eight shown on our map. We were therefore more than a little taken aback when completely out of the blue, we rapidly reached the end of the Bossuit canal and were suddenly facing the 'T' junction with the wide and busy waterway of the Upper Scheldt. Disconcertingly, we had 'lost' two locks. We found out later that the three new locks had replaced five old ones a year after the maps had been printed. Our surreal experience was a salutary lesson in the pitfalls of relying on out-of-date maps.

Turning right at the 'T' junction to head eventually towards the ancient city of Tournai in French-speaking Walloon, we first made for an old quay that we had spotted set back and sheltered off the Scheldt. It had what appeared to be a small hydro-electric station nearby but was otherwise quite remote. With *Snail* safely roped on to the few bollards still useable on this rather dilapidated mooring, Woody scampered off to investigate his new surroundings. After the noise of Kortrijk, this isolated spot was heavenly. There was a narrow lane next to the mooring that followed the edge of the waterway, one way leading to a small village, the other into open countryside. The riverbank opposite was lined with tall poplars as far as the eye could see giving the spot a distinctly French feel. We were almost in Walloon, the southern half of Belgium that had ancient links with France. This would be our last stop in Flanders in the north, allied in the past to the Netherlands and already the differences were palpable.

We were surprised and grateful at how quiet this normally well used waterway was. It would have been a very uncomfortable stop (as we were to find out at a later visit) if there had been a regular volume of barge traffic pushing past. The lockkeeper on the Bossuit told us that an unscheduled waterway stoppage caused by a faulty lock on another canal was diverting many of the barges away from the Scheldt and thus giving us the benefit of an abnormally calm and enjoyable mooring. We savoured two more days of peace here, only occasionally disturbed by the wash from passing barges. They gave us entertainment too as we watched their manoeuvres when reversing off the Scheldt and in to the entrance of the Bossuit, quite a feat with these long and heavy vessels.

The Belgian border between Walloon and Flanders is formed at this point by the Scheldt (known as the Schelde in Flanders and the Escaut in Walloon) waterway. *Snail* was currently moored on the Flemish side. Opposite her amongst the poplars, the river bank was in Walloon. Now underway again, we noticed bridge names that had been 'brug' were now 'pont' and at the next lock, our first in Walloon, Skipper was summoned in a torrent of French to go up to the control tower with our boat's paperwork. This set the scene for many a bureaucratic charade to come and the order of play went something like this:

Control tower window opens and a head appears, barking the command to attend.
Resigned sigh from crew on *Snail*.
Skipper holds paperwork in teeth and carefully ascends slimy lock wall ladder.
Skipper disappears inside control tower, re-appearing many minutes later clasping new paperwork triumphantly.
Hasty descent by Skipper back down slimy ladder in the race to reach *Snail* before tyrant in control tower raises the lock paddles.

We never did find out quite why this rigmarole is insisted upon for pleasure boats at certain locks in Walloon where the computer in the first control tower of a newly entered waterway would churn out reams of paper for Skipper to take back to the boat. When this is demanded to be seen at the next control tower, it is curtly snatched, screwed up and tossed into the waste bin, only to be replaced by another stream of apparently useless computer print-out destined for the same treatment at the next control lock. With no licence needed for your boat in Walloon, all this entertainment is completely free of charge.

While on the Haut-Escaut as the Upper Scheldt was now called, we thought how pleasant it would be to have a bit of a break from the buffeting of the commercial traffic. Again perusing our well-thumbed map, the Espierres Canal with its rural similarity to an English narrow waterway looked just right. If only we had learnt the lesson of the disappearing Bossuit locks when using old maps the following may never have happened. The entrance to this canal was in the middle of what appeared to be a wide turning point on the Haut-Escaut just after our first lock in Walloon, the Ecluse de Herinnes. It would be an easy manoeuvre, even with our 21m. long boat, and Skipper duly turned off the main waterway with me watching up front. Normally I am the first to realise that the bow is not going anywhere. The telltale sounds of crunching coming from under the boat is a giveaway. This time however I heard nothing, apart from shouts from the Skipper who by then, had realised that he too was not going anywhere. The deep mud had stealthily crept up on us. Nothing to worry about, we'd been grounded in England in the past and with me up front to take some weight off the stern and some judicious use of reverse, we'd always got off again. The difference here though was the commercial traffic. Showing no mercy for our predicament, they sped past behind us, each one causing a tidal wave of tsunami proportions that pushed us further and further onto the mud. No amount of reverse engine power was going to get us off this time. We were well and truly stuck!

There followed much contemplation of what to do next. We'd never been in this predicament before. The lockkeeper at Herinnes could still see us from high up in his tower and was chatting on the VHF radio in very fast and to us unintelligible French. The only word we could make out was 'cigar'. How very odd. We hoped he was asking passing vessels to slow down or even perhaps give us a tow off. Quite why any of them, even unladen, would want to chance getting stuck too didn't bear thinking about. It was time for us to be pro-active. Our 'tender' on the *Wandering Snail* is an American plastic folding boat affectionately called *Origami* and normally stored in a box on the roof of the boat. Rugged and stable when put together, she is much more co-operative folding up than opening out so usually we perform this tortuous operation on dry land where there's plenty of room to persuade her to turn into a boat shape. Unfortunately all we had now was the tiny space in *Snail's* bow. If our situation hadn't been so desperate, it would have been 1-0 to *Origami*. By now we had an audience on the banks. We gave them much entertainment as with many expletives, *Origami* was at last put together and launched over the side into the canal. Skipper tied together every rope we could find on board and heroically rowed *Origami* out with it all into the main canal. Here he waved the end of the rope at passing commercials in the hope that one might stop to help, with much encouragement from our audience. At last an empty spits stopped, took the rope and began to pull. The strain of towing a 26ton narrowboat out of its muddy embrace was too much for our ropes which snapped before *Snail* had moved a centimetre. Our audience were getting bored and began to walk away. Skipper gave up too and rowed the valiant *Origami* back, tying her to *Snail's* bow where the next tidal wave capsized her. We had been stranded for 4 hours. Things could not get worse.

Then unexpectedly the fire brigade arrived. They looked at us from the far bank, scratched their heads and said there was nothing they could do. We replied that we couldn't think of anything they could do either and we certainly hadn't called them but they were welcome to stay and keep us company if they had nowhere else to go. Then the chief of Walloon waterways came. This was turning into a party. The fire brigade asked the chief of waterways why there were no warning notices about the lack of depth. Good question, we thought. His reply was that if we'd waited until September, it would have been deeper! We have since learnt that this little canal had attracted European funding to dredge and re-open it as an alternative route between France and Belgium for pleasure boats. At the time of writing the Belgian end that held us fast is now dredged and open but it had not been done in time for the opening ceremony which went ahead that September anyway.

Back to our predicament and there then followed some talk amongst the firemen of getting a tug to pull us off and the awful realisation that if this happened it would not be covered by our insurance. Two more firemen appeared in a little boat to show solidarity we supposed but they kept a careful distance. The *Futura*, all 1500tons of her, decided enough was enough. Miraculously she edged her bows so close to us that Skipper could accept her proffered rope by standing on *Snail's* stern. This commercial rope was as thick as a fist and after some initial reluctance, *Wandering Snail* was at last pulled off the mud. We had been stuck fast for six long, embarrassing and worrying hours and it was now getting dark. Mooring *Snail* safely alongside the lock quay wall back at Ecluse de Herinnes, a kind passer-by helped us pull poor *Origami* out of the water. In spite of it all she was remarkably unscathed. We gave her a good scrub to remove the mud that was caked onto her, packed her back into her roof box and fell into bed.

Stuck in the mud at the entrance to the Espierres Canal.

The oldest bridge on the Tournai one-way system.

The next day after a good sleep we had recovered from our ordeal sufficiently to confidently continue with our journey to the medieval city of Tournai. Centuries before, this city had been the capital of France until that honour was removed to Paris following constant boundary changes and warfare. The waterway that snaked through this ancient place was too narrow for commercial barges to pass each other and so a one-way system operated. We pulled over to wait for our green light and experienced the customary pull on the ropes as the barges came through past us first. Its always fascinating and memorable to approach a city by its waterway. Perhaps because on a narrowboat you invariably have to look up to everything and everyone, it gives each town a lofty appearance. Or maybe it's the very slow pace of boating which allows a gradual and relaxed absorption of atmosphere. Tournai with its rows of ancient waterside buildings and its variety of bridges from antique to modern was a hit with us from the start.

At the end of the one-way section, the city had provided a free pontoon for pleasure boats to stop and explore. We manoeuvred *Snail* into position behind a cruiser already moored and began to rope her up to the T studs provided. This wasn't the most comfortable of moorings with commercial traffic passing very close by but we so wanted to experience this city that we were prepared to put up with the buffeting. We didn't know it then but we would stay here for ten days, a marathon stint compared with the cruisers who came and went after enduring only one night of the discomfort. There had been no-one about as we began to make *Snail* safe but suddenly there was a clatter of stiletto heels on the ramp leading from the pontoon to the road and before we had finished mooring up part of our boat was enveloped in a billowing wedding dress. Its owner was busily draping herself over *Snail* while the rest of the entourage who had followed her down posed unselfconsciously along the pontoon for the accompanying photographer. Open-mouthed we stood with still untied ropes in hand as the party with photos now successfully taken disappeared as rapidly as they had come and with not a word spoken.

Our next visitors were much more effusive. Dominique and his family had seen our arrival from his workshop above the quay wall and had hurried down to look at this 'special' boat. In halting, self-conscious English Dom, as he preferred to be called introduced himself as an eboniste, a craftsman in wood. When he learnt that Skipper had been a cabinet-maker too he immediately invited us to dinner that evening. While we were there he would show us the furniture that he and his wife, also an eboniste, were currently restoring in their workshop attached to the house. So it was that while their lively young children played rather worryingly 'hunt the cat' with our enthusiastic terrier, we enjoyed some delightful company. To make use of their linguistic skills Dom had also invited along Paul, a tutor at the famous furniture making college in Tournai along with his American wife Lauren and also Katherine, the head of the city's tourist service, who had impeccable English. It was the first of many highly sociable evenings during our stay in Tournai with this friendly group of Walloons with whom we discovered many shared interests, not least of which was music making.

The following days were enjoyably spent discovering the city. Grassy parkland edged the perimeter and offered pleasant walks with here and there evidence of the 13th century walls that had once enclosed the town. The many ancient buildings in the middle of the city included the oldest belfry in Belgium and climbing its 257 steps to the top rewarded us with stunning views. The cathedral with no less than five steeple-topped towers dominated the panorama and held the promise of a lofty gothic interior. It would be our next visit. With great anticipation we walked along the old streets that led to the cathedral and stepped inside through the great doors into – a building site. Scaffolding completely filled the interior supporting workmen who were producing noise and dust. There was an archaeological dig in progress that covered the entire chancel floor. Somewhere underneath all this was the gothic masterpiece we had hoped to see but we would have a long wait. The work was estimated to take until 2030 having begun in 1999 following tornado damage although the foundations had apparently been collapsing dangerously for years before.

Our unexpectedly quick visit meant there was time to spare for one of the many tempting Tournai museums. We chose the archaeology museum, there was a certain continuity of theme. The only visitors, we wandered around the floors with the promise of many local artefacts from pre-history to Roman times on display but in reality we found many unexplained spaces in the showcases. We were also uncomfortably aware that we were being followed. By the third floor we'd had enough and asked our unwelcome shadow what was going on. They'd had a robbery, was the terse explanation. Presumably we looked the type. Perhaps it was the cathedral dust still clinging to us but it did explain all the gaps in the showcases.

The Tournai Belfry.

We were sure our day would eventually contrive to end on a high note. There was a free music festival starting that evening and continuing for the next three days at various venues and street corners throughout the city. Dom gave us a programme when we returned to the boat and we arranged to join him and his family the following evening for a tour of the very varied musical offerings. For now we would explore for ourselves but the evening was destined to continue with unfulfilled potential just as the day had done. Each time we came across a venue, the musicians had either just finished and were packing away their gear or a new group were setting up tediously slowly and with interminable sound checks. Time to give up with this day and head for bed. Among the row of buildings near the boat mooring was an intriguing cellar café that had been closed whenever we had passed by. We were almost back at the boat when we realised that now it was open and that there was music coming from inside. Lively and very well played folk music was being performed by a group of students from the furniture making college who had formed a scratch band. We found a table and with our feet tapping and glass in hand, the day was at last retrieved.

Tournai's dragon in front of the cathedral.

Paul had given us tickets for the last concert of the festival which he had been asked to organise. He was an accomplished recorder player as well as a woodwork tutor and we made our way to the venue to enjoy an afternoon of 'musique baroque'. Belgians are not renowned for their timekeeping but when twenty minutes had passed from the advertised concert start time with no sign of it beginning, the audience was getting fidgety. An embarrassed-looking Paul came over to us and confided that the solo violinist had not turned up, could I possibly fill her place? Skipper dashed back to the boat and returned with my violin before I could protest. With explanations to the audience, the concert could at last begin. It turned out to be less nerve racking than I had expected as my totally unrehearsed and therefore much less than perfect performance was excused by the now very sympathetic listeners. As we walked back to the boat, we talked about our enjoyable stay in Tournai that had produced so many memorable and offbeat (in every sense) experiences. It was to remain our favourite Walloon city.

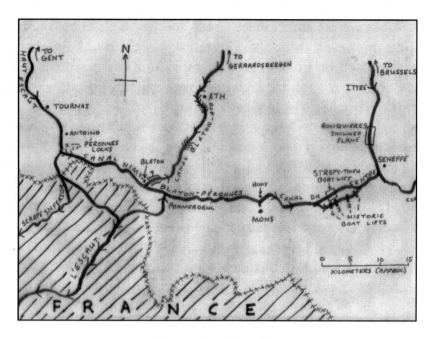

Tournai to Seneffe.

CHAPTER 7.

Antoing to Strepy and back – in which *Snail* goes up in the world.

It was a tough decision for us to move on from Tournai, this ancient city that had so much to offer but there was still a lot of Belgium to see. Dom and Katherine came down to the pontoon to see us off with their children clutching colourful bunches of flowers picked from their garden. Promising to see them again soon we waved goodbye as a gap in the commercial barge traffic gave the opportunity for *Snail* to get under way again. With the next bend of the river the mooring where we had spent the last ten happy days was soon out of sight and mentally we too moved on with renewed anticipation.

A live-aboard life is one of stark self sufficiency. Unless our boat's water tank is regularly filled the taps will produce nothing when turned on. If the diesel tanks are empty the boat cannot move and for us, because we are an 'all diesel' boat, there will also be no heating, lighting or means to cook. Therefore whenever an opportunity presented itself on our travels to obtain these two essentials to our everyday life, we took it. At the town of Antoing not far from Tournai, a 'bunker' barge was permanently moored up and offered diesel and water for sale to passing boats. We roped up to its pontoon and proceeded to fill up our tanks. A large red boat in front of us was doing the same. It bristled with pipe work on its deck and evidently belonged to the bunker barge. They explained that it went out to commercial shipping and coming alongside them would fill their tanks while on the move thus saving them valuable time. With our tanks reassuringly full again we turned onto the Nimy canal and about fifteen kilometres further we took an arm on the left. This was the entrance to the Blaton-Ath canal where we hoped to soon stop for the night. We were looking forward to the Blaton-Ath, a densely locked but little used country canal and rang the contact number displayed on the signboard as we manoeuvred into the arm. This would summon the team of lockkeepers who would take us through over the following days. No reply. Looking at the poor state of the first lock in front of us we wondered if this canal was still operational and with much despondency, we attempted to turn around and leave.

The foul smelling mud that *Snail* churned up followed us back onto the main canal where we found a high wall to moor against for the night. It was a hot June evening with the feel of a storm brewing and as we sat in the bow with a glass in hand the wildlife kept us entertained. There were Daubentons bats skimming the water and plenty of large moths for them to catch. The kingfishers came amazingly close to the boat and so did the largest swimming rats we had ever seen. In hindsight they were probably that inoffensive rodent the orange toothed coypu or maybe even beavers as they are both to be found in this part of Europe. Hastily we went indoors and closed all the portholes just in case they felt like squeezing through to join us while we slept.

After our self imposed hot and airless night we both enjoyed a walk with the dog before we cast off. The towpath we followed soon bore right along the edge of another arm off the Nimy, a very wide waterway called the Pommeroeul canal. We could see that if we had only gone on a little further the day before and turned up this branch instead, we would have been able to moor much more easily on the long waiting quay that led to the first lock of this canal. We chatted to a skipper who had done just that and was now busy sprucing up the paint work on his barge. He told us that the Pommeroeul had been dug in the 70's to create another waterway linking Belgium with France. By the 90's it had already silted up so badly on the French side that it was no longer used. Looking up we could see waterways staff in the high control tower of the first lock. We had no idea what they did all day. This was an amazing waste of a resource but its obsolescence had provided us with a very good mooring opportunity when on the Nimy, a canal that was notably deficient in these and we noted it on our map for future use.

Bunker boat with Neptune ready to leave to fill a commercial while on the move.

Back on *Snail* and we tried to raise the Blaton-Ath lockies one more time but still the phone just rang and rang. There was nothing for it but to continue along the Nimy canal towards the city of Mons where to our dismay the only moorings available seemed to be in an expensive marina noisily situated near a motorway. Grumpily we pulled in and tied up. It transpired that this marina was several kilometres out of town and unusually for Belgium there was no public transport. We reconciled ourselves to the fact that this would be one city we would not be able to visit and introduced ourselves to the boat in front of us, another English couple enjoying the waterways of Belgium. They had good news for us, an up-to-date phone number for the Blaton-Ath canal which was definitely still operational although shallow in places and they showed us their guide book to the Belgian waterways from which they had gleaned the information. It was our first introduction to the work of Jacqueline Jones and her comprehensive manual *'Inland Waterways of Belgium'* (pub. Imray et al) which hastily ordered and sent from England 'poste restante', was to remain our bible throughout the rest of *Snail's* journey. That night it began to rain and showed no sign of easing in the morning. Normally we would have stayed put rather than getting an uncomfortable soaking roping up in the locks that were waiting for us further along the canal. However the thought of the bill we would be presented with if we stayed another day in this elite marina spurred us on and we reached the first of two large locks on what had now seamlessly become the Canal du Centre.

There were many treats in store for us on this canal including four historic boat lifts and the one very modern 'ascenseur' that had been built to replace them but first we had to negotiate the locks. Confidently we entered the first, roped up in the continuing heavy rain and waited for the lock to begin filling with water. Suddenly there was a shout from the lock side and an obviously irate lockkeeper was waving and pointing at us. We had no idea what the problem was. He had come down from his control tower in such a flurry and without his coat that he was like us by now getting very wet and more and more indignant. Slowly we realised he was not going to operate the lock until we had taken in a tyre fender we had inadvertently left dangling. We wondered what reception tyre festooned tug boats got in his lock as the soaked jobsworth climbed back up his tower and finally filled the lock chamber for us. The second lock loomed deep and enormous but it was empty and had the floating bollards set in the lock walls that we found so easy to manage. It was still raining as we waited for the gates to close behind us. Skipper began to yell. Out of the mist loomed the tall bows of an empty commercial barge and it was bearing down on us at a rate of knots. The lockkeeper had flung open his office window and was shouting at us to get out of the way. I've never removed a rope so quickly as we shot forward towards the top lock gates at a speed poor *Snail* had never been asked to achieve before. At the very last moment the barge steered around us and settled on the opposite wall. The panic was over, he'd missed us by a hair's breadth. We reversed back to where we had been and for just a fleeting moment thought of England. What were we doing here? Meanwhile the VHF had come back to life with fast chat in French between the locky and the barge and there was that curious mention of 'cigar' again. Feeling in need of some light relief we pushed on two more kilometres to an old lock set in the right bank that guards the entrance to the Canal Historique du Centre. Here there would be no commercial traffic to grapple with and even better, four wonderful 19th century boat lifts to experience. In we went and with mounting excitement waited for the lock to fill knowing that when the gates opened we would get our first glimpse of these rare structures.

Each of the four boat lifts on this short canal is constructed of an elaborate and stunning geometric lace work of riveted iron girders supporting two counterbalanced water tanks. Each tank takes boats up (or down) a fifteen metre height difference and it's all achieved by pistons and cylinders controlled from machine rooms hidden away in striking and well maintained neo-gothic buildings on the banks. And it all looked unexpectedly familiar. The team who operated these historic monuments appeared pleased to see us and were more than willing to set the lifts in motion just for us. Smoothly and silently the gate across the tank of the first boat lift slid upwards, the red light turned to green and in we went. As we fastened ropes to the bollards provided along the edges of the tank the gate glided down into position behind us again and we were alone in a giant, elaborate bath tub. As we waited to begin the ascent we marvelled at the complex structure containing us. Such an intricate design it must be a nightmare to paint. A siren blared from the machine room on the bank and shattered the peace. We presumed it was a warning that the lift was about to commence its cycle and watched optimistically for signs of movement. The siren wailed again and a member of the operating team approached the lift. He was very sorry he said, but the lift had broken down. Could we reverse out and come back again in a few days time by which time it should be repaired? This day was becoming memorable for all the wrong reasons. Mooring up in the small basin in front of the boat lift we discussed what to try next. It had got too late to move on so we arranged with a member of the staff to stay where we were overnight and then chatted with him about the history of the lifts. We explained that the English canal system has one very similar structure on the River Weaver called the Anderton boatlift. It had recently been rescued from neglect and long term deterioration and was now operational again. Remarkably it transpired that the same Victorian engineer was responsible for all five lifts as he had been invited to Belgium following his success on the Weaver. No wonder it all looked so familiar. That evening as darkness fell the boat lift in front of us was magically and theatrically lit up with subtly changing green and blue lights. It lifted our spirits to be a privileged part of this stage set as we sat outside until late quietly savouring the moment.

One of the four Ascenseur Historique.

The next day was very windy and cloudy, not the best of weather for boating and unseasonable for late June. We decided to stay one more day on this blissfully quiet canal. No other boats came through the lock to join us throughout our stay but there were many passers-by who stared at *Snail*, some with more insistent curiosity than others. Having first read aloud our little 'Please respect our privacy' sign in the workshop porthole, one German-speaking couple spent a while filming us 'close up and personal' regardless. Another American sounding pair had a good long look and then declared the boat to be a caravan. On the whole we found Belgian 'gongoozlers', the British term for these towpath onlookers were unfailingly polite, friendly and less intrusive than other nationalities although we were soon to encounter an unsettling exception to this.

The weather had calmed the following day so back we went through the old lock, filling up our water tank first from the hosepipe dangling on the lock office wall. It didn't really need doing but following our mantra of get it when you can, we thought we should. Out came the lockkeeper with an invoice in 'typical for bureaucratic Walloon' triplicate for the princely amount of three euros, the set charge apparently for a square metre of water. We had only taken a little, just enough to top up the tank so this was very expensive water but we had learnt a lesson. From then on in Walloon we waited until the tank was almost empty before using their three euros worth.

Back on the Canal du Centre we looked forward to experiencing the very modern Strepy-Thieu boat lift. This had been built in 2002 at enormous expense as a quicker alternative to the four Anderton style lifts which a newly dug stretch of canal now by-passed. Astonishingly this vertical lift takes boats up seventy three metres (that's over two hundred and thirty-seven feet) in one breathtaking operation and with the building that houses it standing one hundred and seventeen metres high, it's visible for miles around. The surrounding grass covered hills that had been newly formed from the excavations were planted with rows of neat walnut trees, adding a pleasing sense of symmetry to the perspective and a possible harvest opportunity later in the year. As we approached this towering contemporary structure the lights changed to green and a flashing arrow indicated which of the two available tanks to enter. As so often on our Belgian travels we were all alone and it seemed amazing to us that this gigantic boat lift was going to be operated just for *Snail* and for free. We entered the high-sided tank, roped up and waited. Over one hundred and forty vertical cables each as thick as a man's arm lined the walls around us each with their own sensors and computerised operating box. These cables disappeared upwards to the lofty ceiling very high above our heads. We had never felt so small and insignificant as we watched and waited in this cathedral of a place, floating in a tank of water designed to accommodate one thousand three hundred tonne barges. A loudspeaker blared out a warning and with a whooshing sound, the tank began to glide upwards. It probably took less than ten minutes to reach the top but we were too pre-occupied enjoying the ever changing panoramas as the scenery glided by to notice. As the tank came to a smooth halt at the end of its travel, a pair of sparrow hawks flew out from the roof girders where they had built a nest with a stunning view. Now at the top, the Strepy-Thieu boat lift opened onto a long, straight aqueduct that strode across a valley and afforded the boater yet more glorious views. For us this really was one of the highlights of boating in Belgium.

The Strepy boat lift with the tank on the left of the photo at the top.

There was time to kill before we returned to the Canal Historique and its hopefully by then fully functional historic boat lifts. Following the Canal du Centre for a few more rural kilometres to its junction with the Charleroi – Brussels Canal we found a mooring opportunity for the weekend on the usual 'high for a narrowboat' wall that we'd now come to expect. This one had a small woods behind it that looked very suitable for terrier exploration. It was not to be the quietest of moorings, the locals were too intent on enjoying their free time during what turned out to be a glorious weekend of sunshine for that to happen. Speedboats and water-skiers raced past until dusk fell, causing high waves out of all proportion to the size of their boats. These constantly rocked *Snail* uncomfortably but entertained Woody who has, strangely for a narrowboater, always appreciated speed and watched them intently from the bow. Behind us the woods buzzed annoyingly with the high pitched noise of scrambler bikes enjoying the purpose built trails that we discovered with the dog when at last they had all gone home. The next day we left *Snail* to endure more of the same alone on her wall and walked to the nearby town of Seneffe. By chance that weekend was carnival time in Seneffe with Belgium's usual exuberant and eccentric mix of traditions and costumes. Amongst the giants being pushed along on their hidden wheels, troupes of gilles (a kind of medieval jester) dressed in bulging, over stuffed outfits in the national colours of black, yellow and red with swaying ostrich feather headdresses threw oranges into the crowds. Male moustachioed 'majorettes' in mini skirts swirled through the crowded streets, stopping regularly for refreshment at the beer stalls. Good humoured and welcoming, the people of Seneffe enthusiastically included us in their celebrations.

Monday came and we returned to Strepy, descending in the lift and retracing our way back through the old lock to stop again on the mooring by the first historic lift. It was still not ready for us but we were assured it would be useable in one more day and we were welcome to stay where we were overnight. I went inside to make us coffee leaving Skipper enjoying the sunshine sat on a bench by the towpath. There were the usual amount of gongoozlers as before looking at the boat and Skipper chatted to a middle-aged man who had sat down next to him. He seemed friendly and harmless and I briefly joined them. That evening as we sat in the boat eating a meal *Snail* lurched violently as if someone had stepped heavily on board. We hardly had time to put down our cutlery to investigate when suddenly, standing by the table in front of us inside our boat and smiling broadly, was the man from the bench. Immediately he offered us a present of a rather good bottle of wine so we mentally blamed his impertinence and rudeness on foreign ways and hid our annoyance. By the time we managed to be rid of him he had in very broken English made it clear that he was going to take us to visit Brussels in his car the next evening and insisted I give him our phone number to arrange to meet. Alone again both of us felt too unsettled to risk sitting outside. Neither of us had taken to this man, there was something rather sleazy about him. So instead of enjoying the still warm evening we made sure the doors were locked and feeling strangely isolated and vulnerable for the first time on our journey through Belgium, went to bed.

The knock on the front door in the morning startled both of us after the experience of the night before but it was only a member of the boat lift team with the good news that the repairs were completed and if we would like to make our way again to the boat lift they would take us through. Excitedly we cast off and entered the tank. The unsettling events of last night were put aside as we roped up again and watched the dripping gate descend behind us. A short wait and suddenly we were on the move. Quietly and smoothly the tank was travelling upwards and the buildings on the bank that we could glimpse through the changing gaps in the iron lacework were getting smaller. By the time we had reached the top and left the tank, the lift keeper had raced ahead in his little van to operate the next two swing bridges for us. As we cruised along on this pretty and peaceful canal we realised with astonishment that we were the only boat moving on it in the height of the summer, normally a very busy time on the English canal system, and felt grateful to have been able to have had the experience.

Jolted from our thoughts by the sudden and intrusive ringing of the phone, it displayed an unknown Belgian number. Guessing it was our uninvited visitor from last night I switched the phone off without answering. The lift keeper was suggesting we stopped on this old and rural canal until the next day and by the time we had moored to an out of the way bank side, we had almost put our intruder out of our minds. This was an isolated tree fringed section of the canal with only a few dog walkers passing occasionally. We set out our seats and little folding table on the grassy bank and with the Strepy-Thieu lift on the horizon behind us, enjoyed a warm, relaxing and thankfully undisturbed evening.

When the lift keeper knocked on the door the following morning we were ready to go and looking forward to the next three old 'ascenseurs' that would take us up another forty-five metres to rejoin the Canal du Centre at the other end of this branch. To our surprise, the keeper informed us that there were actually only two more boat lifts to do, after which we had to turn around and come all the way back down again. It was apparently no longer possible to travel the entire canal as there had been a dramatic accident involving a barge which had put the last lift permanently out of action several years ago. This three hundred tonne heavily laden barge had broken its back when the lift malfunctioned, accidentally raising the tank again as the vessel was leaving it. Remembering our own incident with the sirens, it was with anticipation and a tinge of nervousness that we entered the next ascenseur as the gate lifted to accept us but we need not have worried, these marvellous ancient structures worked smoothly and without mishap. The second lift was festooned with young climbers making the most of the opportunities the metal work gave for abseiling and waving enthusiastically as we joined them at the top. At the third we had to wait for two trip boats to emerge from the tank before we could go in – for once we weren't the only boat using this interesting and unique waterway and cheery waves from the trippers as they passed *Snail* added to our enjoyment of this special day.

Near the village of Houdeng-Aimeries and just before the last swing bridge and defunct lift, the keeper suggested we again called it a day. There was a widening of the canal in which we could turn around and the team would return in the morning to take us all the way back down again. We had noted that each boat lift had at least four members of staff attending to its every need. This was an expensive and complicated waterway to keep open and operational and we wondered how it was all funded. Part of the answer was surely the numbers of paying tourists that we had seen on the packed trip boats. Throughout the rest of the afternoon and into the evening a tractor camouflaged as a steam train snaked by regularly behind us on the road pulling a long line of open carriages. It was always full of passengers who had also paid to enjoy the spectacle of this historic canal. As they stared at the unusual sight of an English narrowboat and waved to us sat outside we were sure their contributions were helping to make it possible for us too to be there. It was another warm evening and we had got out the chairs and table again for what would be our last night on this canal. As we sat sipping our drinks we noticed an unlikely quartet on the opposite bank. A pair of mallards, a white goose and a cormorant swam and then left the water to preen together in a line on the grass. They were obviously very happy in each others company and disdainfully ignored Woody's overtures to let him please come over to introduce himself. They were still there the next day dozing in the sun as we prepared to leave. Squeezing diagonally into the last boat lift with a large and very full trip boat we were all entertained by an ascenseur worker who, paintbrush and tin in hand and with no regard for health and safety, was balancing on the top of the tank gate. As the lift descended he quickly painted the girders as they became visible on one side and then when the tank stopped wobbled across to the other side to do the same. He had to paint briskly to keep up as he balanced on the slowly ascending gate as it went up to let us all out. We left the enchanting Canal Historique with broad smiles on our faces.

It was an enjoyably rural cruise for the rest of that day as we returned to the Nimy canal and a late mooring by the time we reached the turn off for the Pommeroeul and the disused lock quay we had spotted an eventful week ago. Held up on the way back at both the commercial locks en route, one with a barge interminably filling his water tanks inside the chamber and the other while surveyors measured the amount of water leakage through the lock gates, it was getting dark as we roped up all alone on the long expanse of quayside on this no man's land of disused canal. The following morning revealed how isolated this wide waterway was. There were no houses or main roads to be seen nearby, just scrub land and trees. A concrete track edging both sides of the canal attracted a few cars and brought anglers to try their luck in the still water. It was all simply heaven for our terrier who frequently took himself off for a cooling dip in the water from a slipway located near the boat.

Maintenance on the Ascenseur.

That evening a cruiser flying a German flag had turned in from the Nimy canal to stop in front of us, perhaps alerted to the ample mooring opportunities by the plume of smoke from our barbeque that we had set up on the quayside to cook the evening meal. The skipper finished tying up his boat just in front of ours and approached us. I offered a friendly greeting which was not returned, instead he asked rather brusquely what time the lock would open in the morning. Blatantly he did not believe me when I explained that it wouldn't be opening at all in the morning as the canal was closed and had been for some years. I watched with astonishment as he then proceeded to walk over to Skipper and asked him exactly the same question. He strode off back to his boat leaving me thinking very evil thoughts about what I would do to him if I had the misfortune to be his wife. We returned to our meal and afterwards sat outside until dark chatting quietly about our varied experiences to date and watching bats swooping around *Snail*.

In the morning the German cruiser had gone but we were not alone. Parked in a line along the canal bank behind us was an assortment of motorhomes all with large, black dogs tied up outside. It was a gathering of the Belgian Newfoundland Club here for the weekend to train their younger dogs to swim and 'rescue' from the slipway that Woody had already discovered. Keeping our eager terrier on a lead, we went over to watch. Several of these beautiful dogs had been untied and were waiting patiently at the top of the slipway. Being very young they seemed oblivious of what was expected of them but we were sure instinct would soon take over. The first training dummy was lobbed into the water and the dogs surged down the slope, ears flapping. At the edge of the water they all stopped dead without even getting their paws wet and looked back at their owners with an unmistakably miserable "Surely you don't expect us to go in there?" expression. Called back to the top again another dummy was thrown in and with lots of loud encouragement the dogs were invited to have another go. Down they all raced again and on reaching the edge as one back they all came. Our terrier could not believe his eyes. What was wrong with these dogs, didn't they know how to swim? We felt it was now time for Woody to show them how it was done and let him off his lead. He raced down the slipway and swum doggedly out to the first dummy, bringing it back before leaping in again to retrieve the second. Unfortunately, true to terrier form he decided he had earned this one and ran off with it, the sound of appreciative applause ringing in his ears. And that was how Woody the terrier became an honorary member of the Newfoundland Club.

Later that day the weather became cooler and the gathering clouds were threatening rain by the time we turned in for the night. The motorhomes had packed up and left and we were all alone again. When we opened the doors the following morning we fleetingly thought we were back on an English canal. For a start it was raining but to complete the picture there in front of us was a narrowboat, the first we had seen since we left England. Over drinks that evening we learnt from its skipper that it had cruised the waterways of Europe for nine summers without mishap and had just returned from Germany. He was single-handing, quite a feat with a long boat when it came to securing in these large locks and we wondered how he managed on his own. The trick apparently was to keep the roof clear so that he could freely and rapidly move along it to secure a central rope. We began to realise how much we relied on the extra storage space offered by *Snail's* long roof which was full with masts, roof boxes and bicycles and she certainly looked very cluttered next to this naked boat. Had we really needed to add all those extras we felt at the time were necessary for boating in Europe when this narrowboat was more than managing with none at all, not even a VHF radio although apparently he was thinking about it.

The next day we said goodbye and went our separate ways. Meetings are necessarily transient with a boating lifestyle but we hoped we would meet him again one day. We were intending to head back to the Bossuit Canal via Antoing and Tournai again to reach the Bovenschelde which would take us back to Gent. It was a gusty day but we had stayed long enough on the Pommeroeul and it was time to move on. Back again at the Peronnes lock where we had been chastised for our naughty fender, we were keen to look professional this time. It really doesn't pay to upset a lockkeeper but he had other ideas when he saw it was us in his lock again. Up went the paddles and he dropped the water level in record speed. Neither of us had time to move our ropes onto the next set of bollards as we rapidly descended and we floundered helpless like inexperienced beginners.

Our day wasn't improved when going under the road bridge at Antoing we experienced the first of only two episodes of vandalism directed specifically at us in all our Belgian cruises. A falling pot of geraniums that had been removed for the purpose from the bridge's floral display came crashing down next to me, narrowly missing my head and as I looked up two boys ran away over the bridge. The mooring near to Antoing's bunker boat seemed secure enough and the town itself was very pleasant with its cobbled streets, a well maintained chateau surrounded by medieval walls and yet more geraniums in hanging baskets providing bright colour in the market place. Moving on to Tournai the next day, we were joined on the city pontoon by a smart Dutch cruiser. The friendly owners asked us about our experiences on the Strepy boatlift and we told them about the views and the pair of sparrowhawks that had flown away at the top. As is often the way, they had a very good grasp of English and seemed to understand, smiling effusively. It was not until we checked with our Dutch dictionary later that we realised they had thought we had seen a pair of flying ferrets.

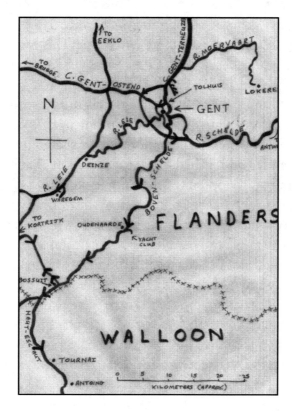

Tournai to Gent.

CHAPTER 8.

Oudenaarde and back to Gent – in which *Snail* and her crew go
back in time and get festive.

The river cruise from Tournai to Oudenaarde brought us back over
the dividing line between Walloon and Flanders. The names of the
towns that we passed reflected the change in language as did the
waterway which began our trip as the very French 'Haut Escaut' and
becoming the equally Flemish 'Bovenschelde' by the time we had
stopped at the historic town of Oudenaarde. On the way we took the
opportunity to meet up with Francis from Kortrijk again by mooring
overnight near the Bossuit canal. He visited us by car, bringing more

local beers for Skipper's delight and fresh brown eggs from his chickens for mine. The last time we had used this mooring the river was quiet and calm because of a diversion. This time it was back to normal and the buffeting from the frequent and all night traffic resulted in a bouncy evening meal. Francis didn't seem to mind but we crossed it off our map as a suitable mooring.

Through driving rain the next morning we shared the Bovenschelde with the big stuff and reached Oudenaarde. Here, having had our fill of barge buffeting, we opted for the calm if expensive at a euro a metre waters of the yacht harbour instead of the bumpy although free riverside quay wall. The yacht harbour was situated at the end of a rather narrow arm off the main river and as soon as we entered it we realised we would not be able to turn *Snail* around to come out again. We hoped the wind had dropped by the time we left as reversing was not one of *Snail*'s strong points and there were many boats to avoid in this busy harbour. The club was friendly and had room for us to stay for a few days so when we heard that there was a very special festival happening over the weekend we decided to hang the expense and stop for a while.

On our approach to Oudenaarde earlier in the day we had noticed from the river a large, dog-friendly field behind the towpath on the edge of town. It was sometimes difficult to find a suitable exercise area for our terrier when we stopped in built up surroundings and this field looked ideal. Giving up waiting for the rain to stop we took Woody for his evening walk back to the river, across the road bridge to the opposite bank and along the towpath that led to the field and terrier paradise. However events had conspired that he never did get the promised run and we were certainly not prepared for the sight that met our incredulous eyes. In the space of an afternoon and while we had been mooring up what had been an empty grassy meadow had been transformed into a bustling 18th century army camp. The field was now covered in rows of white cloth tents, wagonloads of cannons and a hundred grazing horses. Groups of beautifully costumed, be-wigged men with swords at their hips stood around chatting. Others sat outside their tents polishing their guns or combing their wigs. We peeped inside a tent which glowed with pewter utensils and candlesticks but what really caught our eye was the replica wooden folding furniture. This included an ingeniously designed and very comfortable looking double bed. The degree of authenticity was astonishing and we were immediately and convincingly transported back in time. Exactly three hundred years ago one of the many battles for Belgium then known as the Spanish Netherlands, had taken place here in Oudenaarde. The conflict had involved many countries who sided either with the French army led by the Duke of Burgundy or the British led by Churchill, Duke of Marlborough. Or like the Irish and the Scots, fought for whoever paid them the most. Churchill had emerged victorious on the day and it was this battle that was to be re-enacted in Oudenaarde over the weekend to mark its three hundredth anniversary.

Flags from the various European countries taking part hung down damply in the continuing rain from high poles set around the site but with these clues to follow through the crowded bivouac we were able to see the English contingent near the river edge and made our way there. As we approached the British camp two disreputable looking women came over and introduced themselves. Clare and Theresa were hangers-on with the British army, known in the 18th century as the 'baggage'. They provided a mobile shop selling little luxuries such as salt fish, sugar and presumably anything else if asked to make the soldier's life a happier one. These two enthusiastic re-enactors offered us spare costumes and we were enlisted there and then to join the baggage contingent for the next day's parade through the town and on to the battleground.

We eventually tore ourselves away and wandered back to the road bridge musing over this unexpected turn of events and loving Belgium for its eccentricities and joie de vivre. When we reached the bridge the barriers were down across the road as if a barge was about to come through and we waited with everyone else for the bridge to be raised. It was rush hour and the traffic had built up, the tailbacks filling the roads as far as the eye could see. The bridge only went up about three foot and then stopped. Two workmen strode over with paint brush and tin and began to carefully paint the exposed length of bridge. With amazing good humour everyone waited. Some drivers got out of their cars and seeing what was happening, passed the time of day with their neighbour. Pedestrians looked on bemused as the men got on with the job in hand. Eventually the work was finished, the bridge dropped back in to place and everyone was on the move again. At no time had anybody sounded their horn or displayed any sign of frustration. Perhaps it was because the rain had at last stopped.

The next day Oudenaarde was packed with visitors who had all come to see the spectacle on the field by the river. Dressed in our borrowed costumes it was easy to forget the 21st century as we mingled with the foot soldiers and admired the elaborate uniforms of the cavalry as they exercised their glossy horses. There were many hundreds of participants speaking several different languages and it took some organising to muster everyone ready for the parade. This would take us through Oudenaarde's market place and past its ornate gothic town hall where the mayor would wave us on from the balcony. Crowds of people lined the route to watch the armies pass by and television cameras recorded the colour, noise and splendour of it all as we processed to the battlefield. Here the cannons that had been pulled along on handcarts were assembled at each end of the field along with the opposing armies who lined up their musket fire. The rest of us watched from what we hoped would be a safe distance and the battle commenced. As this was after all only a re-enactment of the actual event we had not anticipated the very realistic, ear-splitting, building-shaking boom of the cannons. Perhaps we should have done, having seen the attention to detail so far. It was all too much for Woody's sensitive ears and he began to howl with pain and fright. Our normally fearless terrier had to be carried through the smoke-filled arena and back to the boat where he did eventually recover his composure but that spelt the end of our foray into the 18th century.

Back in the present and it was time to move on, taking advantage on this normally heavily used waterway of the peaceful boating that a Sunday often offered. It was traditionally the commercial barges day off and the Bovenschelde was blissfully quiet as we returned on it to Gent. There are many small medieval canals that weave through and around this old city. Several are now closed to navigation, some are only open to trip boats and small craft but there remain a few canals that are suitable for *Snail* to use. We decided there was still time to reach Tolhuis, our preferred mooring on the edge of the city by taking a more convoluted route using some of these ancient canals with the added attraction of discovering some of the older outskirts of Gent. The trip boats were out in force this sunny Sunday afternoon, their skippers looking surprised to meet another boat on these often deserted backstreet canals and their passengers smiling, waving and taking photos of *Snail*. Many of the banks were lined with ivy clad walls of mellow brick containing the gardens of waterside period houses and old barges converted to live aboard homes also dotted the route with colourful flowers and herbs grown in a variety of pots on their decks. We motored slowly past, enjoying the warm sunshine and absorbing the atmosphere of this forgotten part of Gent.

Waiting for the re-enactment at Oudenaarde to begin.

Our timetable for the rail bridge that barred our way to the mooring at Tolhuis showed that we would just make the last opening of the day so we were surprised when we reached it to see red lights and a firmly closed bridge at the time it was supposed to be open. We decided that the bridge keeper had assumed there would be no more boat traffic at that time on a Sunday and had gone home for an early tea. Luckily there was just enough space along the bank before the bridge for us to squeeze in between some more live aboard boats and we stopped for the day. Skipper took the opportunity to finish the wooden 'dragon' he had been making on and off over the past weeks. Inspired by the belfry dragon weathervanes of Gent and Tournai and the solitary one on the Moervaart tower, Skipper's was beautifully carved with a long curling tail to catch the wind. It looked stunning in its new coat of gold paint.

Before we left the next day our Belgian dragon was in position on the roof at the front of the boat ready for a special trip back along the Moervaart to Lokeren. Here we had promised to give support to Fernand in his quest to re-open navigation through the town. To raise awareness of the benefits that a re-instated river route from Lokeren to Antwerp would bring, Fernand had tempted the Belgian Minister of Transport to visit the town for the day arriving in some style on the fabulous gilded Gentse Barge. This was a faithful replica of an 18th century royal ship built by unemployed youngsters to teach them new skills and was now used for prestigious occasions in and around Gent. *Snail*, specially cleaned and polished for the occasion joined the flotilla as it weaved its way around the bends of the river Moervaart with the bridge keepers looking suitably dapper in their best uniforms and saluting crisply for the benefit of the TV cameras as we passed through. It was all very jolly.

At Lokeren we moored at a respectful distance from the splendid barge whose distinguished occupants were then disembarking. Some of the dignitaries came over to speak with us and it was then that we discovered that Belgian politics, which were forever it seemed to us in a state of extraordinary flux had dealt Fernand a disappointment. The prime minister had that very day tendered his resignation to the king and all the top ministers had been called back to Parliament. That summons had included the Minister for Transport who had instead sent an underling to take his place. Unfortunately for Fernand's hopes, this stand-in had little influence. There is still no through route by boat for Lokeren and the town remains the end of navigation although Fernand continues to promote the issue and certainly hasn't given up hope.

Our completed dragon on the Moervaart.

While in Lokeren we took the opportunity to introduce ourselves to the generous boater who had offered through Anne and Hendrik to let us moor alongside him for the winter. Wim welcomed us on board his large red barge where we sat outside on the wide deck in the late evening sun. Over a bottle of wine we discovered a little more about this kind hearted, quietly spoken, middle aged Belgian. Monday to Friday Wim worked as a taxi driver in Antwerp. His free time however was devoted to a hobby for which we came to realise during that first winter this un-assuming man was much sought after. Wim was a celebrated tango dancer with a long list of ever hopeful potential dancing partners he could call on. You could have knocked us down with a feather.

The next day Fernand brought us some post from England that he had kindly agreed to have sent to him. Needing a better arrangement for the coming winter that would not involve bothering our newly made friends, I walked to the town's large post office. It was very busy with all the counters staffed and occupied with customers but eventually it was my turn and I asked in what I hoped was careful and slow English how to set about having a temporary P.O.box. My request was greeted with a quizzical look from behind the glass partition so I tried again. The assistant's English was evidently not up to the job and she leant over to ask her colleague in the next booth to help. I explained it all over again but still with no response. This assistant then asked in a loud voice if any of the other cashiers could make out what I was trying to say. The queue of customers in the post office was growing and so was my discomfort as all the staff stopped serving to mull over my request. My embarrassment was complete when the manager came over to see what all the fuss was about and eventually told me that no, it was not possible to have a P.O.box without a Belgian address. As I turned to find my way back through the long queues to the door, a young man at the next counter whose transactions had been interrupted when all the staff had had their palaver on my behalf, offered to help. Intrigued and not a little flattered by his use of 'Miss' to gain my attention, I waited for him to finish. Timothy introduced himself saying he knew how difficult receiving post could be as he had travelled widely outside of Belgium but if we trusted him we could use his Lokeren address. His house was only a short walk from the boat and he would drop off anything that arrived for us in the mornings on his way to work. Fleetingly I remembered the disturbing encounter we had had with the stranger on the boat the previous month which had indeed made us less trusting. Pushing these unpleasant thoughts aside, annoyed with the enduring and uncomfortable effect that experience continued to evoke, I gratefully took the young Belgian up on this typically generous offer. It was the start of another enduring friendship.

The next day would be an anniversary of our live aboard life and to celebrate we wanted to cook a favourite meal of roast lamb. It's an expensive meat in Belgium but remembering Anne's advice about using Turkish owned shops, I said goodbye to Timothy and made my way to the one in Lokeren. Thankfully the butcher there spoke very good English and had no difficulty at all in understanding my request for a leg of lamb. He smiled broadly and disappeared into the back of the shop to find me he said a very fresh piece to enjoy. The little Turkish butcher soon returned staggering under the weight of an entire sheep with its legs pointing up to the ceiling. Which one would I like he asked with a completely straight face.

The 165th Gentse Feesten was due to start in two days time and we had promised Rik and Nelly we would be there. In yet more rain we returned on the peaceful Moervaart River past the stork nest which by now was home to three storklings and on to the hectic Gent-Terneuzen Canal where the frequency of overtaking barges caused long lasting deep and choppy waves that left a greasy diesel deposit on *Snail's* gunwales and bow. The mooring quay at Tolhuis, normally fairly empty was already full of boats who had also come to Gent for the famous yearly extravaganza of music and theatre. We managed to moor in the only space left. It was really too short but no-one seemed to mind that our stern was sticking out a little. That afternoon a spits' skipper decided to stop and enjoy the entertainment too. There was absolutely no space left but he manoeuvred until he could moor alongside the barge behind us. The vast propeller visible above the waterline on his unladen spits was now spinning worryingly close to our protruding rear. We tightened the ropes, hoped for the best and took the tram in to the city.

Preparations for the start of the festival the following day were well advanced. All over the city temporary stages and seating had been set up. They were to be found in market squares, in front of churches and in the parks. The most impressive however was an imposing dome-shaped arena bristling with spotlights that spanned the ancient Graslei Canal in the middle of Gent and which would be the main stage for the festival's top performers. On the canal itself, substantial floating pontoons had been tied to the quays and were covered in café style tables and chairs. They took up most of the canal but left just enough room for the trip boats to squeeze through and continue their popular tours of the city's waterways. Along the Graslei the medieval facades of the stone houses that lined both sides of this ancient waterway were now hidden behind brightly coloured temporary bars, restaurants and market stalls. Workmen were everywhere, beavering away to have everything ready for the hundreds of thousands of people who would fill the city over the next ten days. That evening we got *Origami* out of her roofbox and put her together on the quayside. We had often talked about taking our little boat around the Gent canals that were too small for *Snail* and now with the added bonus of the festival seemed a good time. We tied her securely to *Snail* and hoped the rain would be finished by the following morning.

Day one of the festival dawned dry and warm. Rik and Nelly offered to come with us in *Origami* to help us find our way around the elaborate canal network. They had brought a map with them as their plans for the day included mooring by a favourite beer café that had live jazz on the terrace all afternoon and they didn't want us to lose our way in the maze of waterways. Using our portable VHF radio we called up Tolhuis lock, the first obstacle to entering the canal system of Gent. Red lights turned to green as the mighty gates of this commercial sized lock opened to let little *Origami* in. We waved to the lockkeeper high above us in his tower, feeling embarrassed and more than a little apologetic that he would have to work the lock just for our tiny boat. The next obstacle was the water police. They were waiting in a high speed Zodiac to intercept boats that like us hoped to access the festival by navigating the inner city canals. Rather curiously they wanted to know if we had another, bigger boat and as the trip boats manoeuvred around us we explained about our narrowboat moored in Tolhuis. On hearing this they let us carry on, wishing us a good festival. Puzzled, we thanked them and made our way at last to the Graslei canal. On the way Rik explained that the police were checking licences. Our tender did not need one once they had established we had another licensed boat, hence the question.

As we explored the city canals the festive atmosphere was carried to us on the water by the sight of the crowds and the sounds of the music. The great stage over the Graslei was reverberating to the reggae beat of the band that was playing above us as Skipper steered *Origami* underneath and out the other side. The Gentse Barge that we had last seen in Lokeren was moored to a quay wall opposite the canal side café that Rik and Nelly had recommended and where the jazz band was already playing. Little *Origami* snuggled in behind the Barge next to some conveniently placed stone steps and we all climbed out to spend the rest of that happy afternoon dancing and drinking. It was consequently with some difficulty that our little boat's crew tried to negotiate the lock on their return that evening.

A giant at the Gentse Feesten.

Hot air balloon over our mooring at Tolhuis.

The festival continued for another nine days, each of them offering twenty four hours of free music and theatre all over the city. We lasted just five, eventually finding the crowded streets, however good humoured, all a little bit too much. For us the best experiences of the festival came from the spontaneity and exuberance of unofficial street corner scratch bands. It was always a joy to round a corner and discover that there was yet another group of often very talented musicians taking the opportunity to have fun and make impromptu music together at this extraordinary event. On our last evening back at Tolhuis after another musical feast of a day, five hot air balloons taking advantage of a gentle breeze hung in the sky low over the boats. It was an elegant and calming finish to another memorable Belgian week.

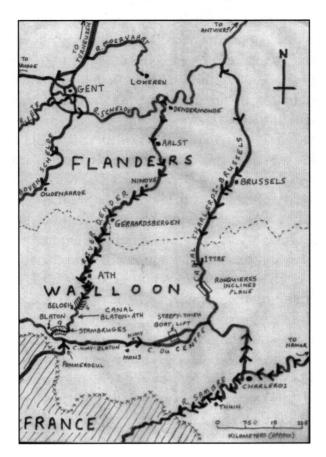

Gent to Ronquieres.

CHAPTER 9.

Dendermonde to Ronquieres – in which Snail goes on the rails.

Now armed with up-to-date contact and operating details gleaned from our ever-useful 'Jones' guide book, it was time to attempt the Blaton-Ath canal again. Coming from Gent, we would now approach it from the other end still in Flanders beginning at Dendermonde lock on the river Dender. This river would then seamlessly become the Blaton-Ath canal when it reached the border with Walloon. There was two hours of the tidal Zeeschelde to do first and being a weekday we had our fair share of commercial traffic to look out for. We were all hoping to save some diesel by catching the tide at the exact time as it went out to sea again. As this was the direction we were travelling in, the river would take us along with it too. The tricky bit would come when manoeuvring *Snail* sideways against the current to turn off at the Dender junction. If you were really skilled you would time this for when the tide was slack just before it began to return again from the sea. Being inexperienced, we were not yet that clever and prayed the lock was already open for us to slip into rather than having to wait outside treading water in the strong current while the lockkeeper prepared it. Our prayers were answered, we entered the tidal lock without a hitch and were soon emptied out onto the non-tidal River Dender. We had been very aware while on the Zeeschelde of non-stop motorway traffic running parallel with the river. It was partly hidden by rows of trees which also obscured many derelict industrial buildings. It was not the prettiest waterway in Belgium. The River Dender, so close to the 'Schelde but so different was immediately rural and quiet and we had the feeling we were going to enjoy this waterway.

The next lock along the river was called Denderbelle. It was already open for us and we hoped to stop overnight just the other side once through. The lockkeeper came out of his office to say hello, help with our ropes and agree that there was no problem for us to stay as long as we wanted. The wooden mooring platform provided by the lock exit was empty. It had seen better days and being careful where we put our feet we roped up to the more secure looking bollards of a wobbly selection. By the time we had done, the Denderbelle lockkeeper had finished for the day too and walked over to have a chat. We had already noticed that he was unusually slim and well dressed for a lockkeeper. With perfectly coiffured hair and tiny chihuahua tucked under his arm the picture was complete. We were no longer surprised at the unusual name for his lock or to come across the only pink bridge in Belgium on this stretch of river when we moved on. In a previous life this lockkeeper had been a masseuse for the Tour de France cycling team (no surprise there either) and he warned us to keep Woody on a lead as the towpath was used regularly for training. We had noticed while we chatted that behind him speedy lycra-clad teams were whizzing by and apparently if we were still here on a Sunday there would be many thousands of them passing our boat by the end of the day. At least they wouldn't have time to stare at us. The next day the sun shone and as it was the only time that summer when we had had two sunny days in a row (it was now the end of July) we decided to stay for one more day and walk through the fields to the villages on either side of the river. Numerous cyclists had already sped past by the time we had finished breakfast. Young and old, fat and thin, some lycra-clad in team colours and all this on a week day. Didn't anyone work around here? By night fall it was peaceful and we had the river to ourselves again. There had been no other boats passing us in the two days we had spent here although the lockkeeper had put through another narrowboat once before. Owned by an American couple and flying an Hawaiian flag, we got the feeling he considered it much more exotic than poor *Snail*.

We moved on the next day to stop at the town of Aalst. A mobile team of lock and bridge staff cheerfully attended to our needs and suggested we moored against a wall in between the two town bridges. It was a little high for a narrowboat but we were getting used to that now. Rain was again threatening as we found our way late in the morning into the old town to catch the market before it closed. It was a picturesque sight with the colourful stalls spread along the narrow streets and medieval market place of Aalst. We would have stayed longer if the storm had held off. With heads down against the wind and rain we raced back to the boat. Over a comforting coffee we peered out through the drenched side hatch windows at the boats in the yacht club opposite. Looking wet and miserable on the grass behind the moored cruisers was a ragged group of very free range chickens. They were to give us comic entertainment that night as they tried with varying degrees of nimbleness to leap up into the branches of the willow trees to roost. This mongrel assortment of poultry postponed their revenge for us laughing at them until the early hours when we were woken by the calls of the wild cockerels who made sure we slept no more that night. We would have liked to have seen a little more of Aalst but not with such noisy neighbours. In the morning we called up the team to say we would be on the move and said goodbye to the chickens.

Aalst

On the edge of Aalst by the river stands the biggest sugar refinery in Europe. As we cruised past this shiny steel giant we were surprised to see a reminder of England, the sign outside proclaimed it to be owned by Tate and Lyle. Soon leaving industry behind, the river followed a beautiful course. Under-used like so many of Belgium's waterways, it was a haven for wildlife and we saw the first of many kingfishers disappear into the reeds ahead of us. The lockkeeper pottered along the towpath on his scooter and stopped to suggest we stayed overnight before the bridge at Ninove. Apparently the yacht club there was closed but the moorings were still useable and so we agreed. While we secured *Snail*, our eccentric looking locky complete with handle-bar moustache chatted about our arrangements for tomorrow. His fluent English was well enunciated in a booming, deep bass voice. Without much prompting he spoke to us proudly of his achievements in the world town-crier championships and the reason for his whimsical appearance became clear. He told us in a much quieter and conspiritorial voice about the fate of the yacht club, closed because of "financial irregularities". We wondered if it would ever open again, its clubhouse was already looking very uncared for as we called "Tot ziens, see you tomorrow." to this larger than life character now back on his scooter ready to go home.

A few yards from the boat there was an attractive public park with some old specimen trees and a small lake. Before we had the chance to take a stroll through its invitingly cool and shady greenery, a bridal party who had seen us from the bridge descended on *Snail*. As at Tournai nothing was said, no permission asked for and the photos were taken as if we, the owners of this unusual backdrop were invisible. I rushed back inside the boat to fetch our camera and just had time to take a snap of the voluminous bride with her equally voluminous dress sweeping back along the pontoon, her mission accomplished.

Apologies to Ninovians but I think they would agree that Ninove town is a non-descript sort of place so we gladly moved on the next day with our hirsute locky in attendance racing on his moped to have the locks and bridges open for us. We wished he would go a little slower. This was a stretch of river not to be rushed as it wound its peaceful way in the hot sunshine to the hills of Geraardsbergen, the old town where we would stop next. Squeezing *Snail* into a gap between the town lock and the start of expensive marina pontoons, we risked using mooring pins on this non-commercial river for the first time since arriving in Belgium and hammered them into the grass bank. We had to climb up a slope to get out but at least it was free.

Geraardsbergen turned out to be a beautiful city, for that was what its inhabitants called this compact town. We explored its delightful steep and narrow streets and the pretty market square with a 'Pissing Boy' statue that the town claims to be older than the more famous Brussels equivalent. They argue still, keeping the feud between Flemish and French speakers in Belgium alive and well. Geraardsbergen is on the Tour de France route and is well known for the steep and cobbled hill section that takes the cyclists high up over the town. Known as the

Muur, the wall, we pitied the competitors as we staggered up to the top. The views were wonderful but presumably the racing cyclists didn't have time to appreciate them. Returning to the town, we enjoyed a restorative beer in a café overlooking the river before returning to the boat. While we had been away a new lockkeeper had arrived and was looking inquisitively at *Snail*. He explained that he would not be accompanying us onward as tomorrow we would be crossing the dividing line and entering the waterways of Walloon. Here the same channel that was a river in Flanders becomes a canal in Walloon, the Blaton-Ath, and we would need to call up a new team of French speaking lockies before we could continue.

The 'Pissing Boy' statue at Geraardsbergen.

The Blaton-Ath canal was every bit as lovely as the River Dender had been. The cruise to the town of Ath was delightful and featured some curious sights. In a canal side field an antiquated Dakota aeroplane had long ago been abandoned and was left bizarrely stranded, surrounded by grazing cows. Further on, a paddock attached to a canalside cottage contained a fanciful collection of ostrich, goat and wild boar which made a change from ducks and chickens. The grassy quayside at Ath provided a good mooring for Woody and crew alike and before he left us to discover the town the lockkeeper gave Skipper a leaflet about the canal that had been carefully 'translated' into English. It contained lots of useful boaty information including the puzzling instruction not to lie in the middle of the road. Bearing this in mind we left *Snail* and found the way into the town. Ath had plenty to keep us interested. There was a good local beer that could be enjoyed at any of the continental style cafés in the medieval surroundings of the market square and the locals were friendly and hospitable. There were two museums, one of which celebrated the Belgian carnival tradition of giants made in wickerwork. For us however the most absorbing visit in Ath was to the Gallo-Roman museum. When the now defunct Pommeroeul canal was dug out in the 1970's, it rapidly became apparent that the Romans had been there first using the same course for a canal of their own over two thousand years before. So many finds were excavated from the site that a museum was set up in Ath solely to exhibit them and among the many well preserved artefacts all imaginatively presented here were two beautiful and remarkably intact wooden Roman barges.

The next few days saw us negotiating ten locks interspersed with swing bridges all operated efficiently for us by two teams of keepers working in relay. To begin with we were in the company of a couple of friendly Dutch cruisers but they soon sped on their way leaving *Snail* alone again. It was now August and we never ceased to be amazed at how quiet the waterways were in Belgium in the summer. One evening we unwisely chose to stop by a swing bridge at Beloeil. The château of that name near the village charged a high entrance fee, too expensive to consider on our meagre budget and the bridge clattered noisily every time a vehicle went over it which was uncomfortably often. Much more to our taste was the extensive forest that we found further along the canal at Stambruges. Thickly wooded with shadowy paths leading in to the dark depths from the tree-lined mooring, we spent three happy days exploring. There was also a quaint village within walking distance from the boat mooring where the general store had not changed in style for decades. The marble counters and dark wood shelves were stocked with locally made delicacies. As a result, flavourful salamis and local beers accompanied freshly made artisanal bread for our daily picnics enjoyed in sun-dappled clearings in the forest where red squirrels in the surrounding trees kept Woody amused.

Back at the boat still in this lovely spot there was a knock on the open hatch and a plate of freshly cooked pancakes appeared. A large Belgian boat with a young family on board had moored in front of us and this was their delightful way of introducing themselves. Later we were all joined by a local couple who stopped on the towpath to talk to the crews of the two boats that had chosen to stop in their neck of the woods. The highly sociable evening that ensued resulted in a gift of local beer brought to the boat the next day and an offer of a guided walk through the forest. This knowledgeable pair were keen to show us La Mer de Sable, an ancient inland sea that had dried up long ago. Now all that was left was a vast sandy, open area incongruously situated in the depths of the forest. Promising ourselves we would come back again one day to this lovely waterway, we reluctantly left Stambruges to cruise on towards the end of the canal at Blaton. A further ten locks were operated cheerfully by a team of three staff racing ahead on their scooters, all demonstrably very happy in their work on this summer's day. In return for cups of coffee our water tank was filled for free while we were going up in one of the locks. Just before we went through the last they suggested we stopped to enjoy one more night on this quiet canal using the offside bank instead of the well walked and busy towpath side opposite. They would return to take us through the last lock in the morning. As we moored up among the wild flowers growing in the grass along the canalside, Woody grabbed the opportunity to swim in the clear water. Here on the offside of the canal no-one disturbed us and we set up a last barbeque under a spreading walnut tree, hanging lanterns from its branches as dusk approached. It was difficult to imagine the wide, busy commercial canal that was waiting for us the next day just the other side of that last lock.

Lockkeepers on the Blaton-Ath Canal.

Surrounded by debris and the stench from the mud that our propeller was churning up, we remembered that this had been our introduction to the Blaton-Ath canal junction nearly two months before. Then we had turned back having failed to raise the lockkeepers and little knowing of the delightful waterway that was hidden behind the tall gates of the lock. Now with the experience still very fresh in our memory we had to return to more usual Belgian boating on wide canals looking out for the big stuff. Over the next three days we made our way back via the Pommeroeul mooring and Mons to the Canal du Centre and the Strepy boatlift again. The journey was unexpectedly quiet with very few commercial barges on the move. This provided a pleasant, gradual adjustment that we were thankful for and we stopped on the third afternoon of the trip by the boatlift at Strepy. Here we moored with only two other boats on the long expanse of mooring wall with Woody keen to go climbing the landscaped hills. We were happy to oblige but as I waited in the bow for Skipper to join us, I noticed a man standing a few yards away watching our boat. He looked uncomfortably familiar. I stepped back inside quickly but knew he must have seen me. With a sinking feeling I warned Skipper that the unpleasant Belgian was back. There was nothing for it but to continue with our dog walking plans or stay trapped inside the boat. It meant we would have to pass the man but perhaps he had gone by now. We locked the doors and stepped outside. He was waiting for us. He looked angry and asked why we had ignored his phone call. We made an excuse but kept walking and, scooping up a confused terrier strode purposefully into the Strepy boatlift exhibition centre. The tall glass doors slid shut behind us and the man stayed outside for a moment then walked away. We waited until he had got into his car and driven off before we dared to leave the building and give Woody his long awaited hilltop walk.

Equanimity and humour were soon returned as we set off the next morning and a tiny cruiser shot in front of us grimly racing to get to the boatlift first. Apart from us there was nothing else waiting to use it and the absurdity of this unnecessary manoeuvre faced with the yawning emptiness of the boatlift tank made us smile wryly. The weather when we reached the top of the lift tried to depress us again. It was grey and wet but we were full of excited anticipation. We were on our way to another of Belgium's famous waterway structures, the inclined plane at Ronquieres.

A tank at Ronquieres Inclined Plane coming up for us.

Built in the early 1960's to replace fourteen locks, Ronquieres' tanks can hold one thousand three hundred and fifty tons of boat. These are water filled as at Strepy but unlike the boatlift are instead moved up and down on rails fixed to the hillside. Each tank sits on two hundred and thirty-six wheels which give a reasonably smooth ride as you are winched along. We had been warned that there were often long delays as commercial barges waited their turn to use the inclined plane on this busy waterway that linked industrial Charleroi with Brussels and the Zeeschelde. But this was a Sunday and as we approached, the only other vessel we could see that was also on the move was an empty trip boat. We both went straight in to the waiting tank, the gate slid down behind us and with eerie moanings and groanings the wheels and winches began to turn. It was a long, slow descent giving us plenty of time to admire the views. The sight far below of a car driving along towards us in the gap between the two sets of rails was a little distracting. Perhaps he was blindly following the instructions from his GPS? Equally diverting was the spread-eagled figure of a man outlined in white paint far below us on the ground in a 'forensic' style. It became more visible as we approached the end of the tank's travel but nobody else seemed concerned. Well, this was Belgium after all. We moored at the bottom of the inclined plane among a line of commercial barges and wandered off to pick wild mint and hazelnuts, both growing in profusion along the towpath.

It had been an interesting day and we had plenty to talk about as we relaxed inside *Snail* later with our evening meal. So relaxed that we were totally unprepared for the violent lurching of the boat immediately followed by the sudden appearance of the unpleasant Belgian who quickly joined us at the table with a self-satisfied smile. Ignoring his attempts to engage us in conversation and wishing our terrier wasn't quite so frenetic in his welcome (he loves visitors without discrimination) this disagreeable man eventually said goodbye and left. We locked the doors behind him and sat down, stunned. How had he known where to find us? Had he a friend on the waterways keeping him informed? We would never find out but knew now what it felt like to be stalked and it was very unpleasant. The following few days were marred by always remembering to keep the doors locked and worrying about where this individual would appear next but we were determined not to be forced to leave this otherwise attractive area. We stayed to enjoy the village of Ronquieres with its ancient watermill and pretty church and then moved on to Ittre lock, at fourteen metres probably the deepest in Belgium. Here there were no available moorings and the lockside water supply didn't fit our hosepipe so reluctantly we decided to risk a return to Ronquieres. There the lift was operated just for us and it all seemed even more exciting than before as the tank was slowly and noisily heaved up the sixty-eight metres to the top. Neither of us could face the anxiety of another evening spent at Ronquieres and we pressed on towards Charleroi, hoping this would be far enough away to discourage our stalker. We finally stopped at the end of a long day at the first of the three locks before the city. We were now very close to industry and urban sprawl. In front of us was a motorway, behind us a railway and overhead jets added to the constant hum. A huge four storey German ship came past full of holiday makers, reminding us of the inter-connectedness and accessibility of Belgium's waterway network. Nevertheless this was a pretty, rural spot and we enjoyed our overnight stay thankfully uninterrupted. Tomorrow beyond Charleroi the waterways would take us to a very different part of Belgium. There was still a lot to look forward to.

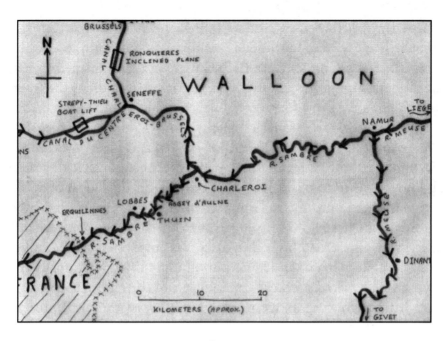

River Sambre to Namur.

CHAPTER 10.

Charleroi and the Sambre – in which we pass through Hades and
into heaven.

Summoned up to the office at the top of the lock control tower, Skipper
had to decide there and then where we were going next. The computer
was waiting as was the lockkeeper and it's a difficult decision when the
lifestyle allows for never having to stick with a plan. Skipper thought
for a moment and then mentioned the River Sambre towards France,
perhaps. That was enough information for the impatient computer to
pounce on and commence its long regurgitation of reams of paper
which although obligatory for all boaters to be issued with in Walloon,
we had so far found absolutely no use for. The bargee standing in the
wheelhouse of a spits full of scrap metal who had been held up in the
lock with us while this bureaucratic charade took place stared ahead

resignedly. It had been his turn first, he knew the drill. With Skipper's decision made to head for the Sambre, this would be for us the last lock on the Brussels-Charleroi canal. Eventually its gates opened to reveal the gloomy beginnings of heavily industrial surroundings that would stretch along the canal for over a mile and which would have made an ideal backdrop for a Charles Dickens novel. Built in the 1880's Charleroi's old steelworks loomed rusty red and filthy, blocking out the light on both sides of the canal. The old, ramshackle factory buildings seemed to be held together only by the thick dust of decades that was caked onto them. Glimpses of glowing furnaces fed by the mountainous heaps of scrap metal that lined the canalside made us realise with a start that this hellish place was not as we had first thought, a museum piece from the 19th century, but a fully operational works. Two grime covered workers emerging from the gloom to raise their hard hats in greeting as we went by confirmed the uncomfortable realisation that while we were enjoying life, some had to spend much of their waking hours in this place. Incredibly, the one and only kingfisher that we were to see in the next weeks shot ahead of Snail as we cruised on through the steelworks and its rust coloured waters.

The 'hell' that is Charleroi Steel Plant.

Reaching the 'T' junction with the River Sambre we did as we had said we would at the lock and turned right towards France. We were soon rewarded for our compliance by enduring what we came to regard as the worst lock in Belgium, Monceau-sur-Sambre. The maelstrom caused by its strange underwater filling system threw *Snail* around unmercifully and all watched by a grinning, unsympathetic lockkeeper. As we hung on with grim determination to our ropes we hoped he would be replaced by a more skilful and thoughtful operator for our return visit but all this was soon forgotten as the lock gates opened and we got our first sight of the river. Rock faced and steeply forested on one bank, hillside farms and fields on the other, the Haute Sambre presented us with the ultimate we were looking for in our boating – peace and beauty. Now the middle of August there was not another boat moving on this beautiful river. This surprised us as apart from the tranquillity it offered this waterway was also a route into that supremely popular pleasure boating country, France.

We stopped for the night near the magnificent ruined abbey of Aulne, a stunning backdrop lit up splendidly by a colourful sunset. The boat attracted a lot of interest that evening from passing locals and from the assorted geese who roamed freely in large and noisy gangs along the river banks. As darkness fell we were left alone to simply revel in these wonderful and atmospheric surroundings. By the 18th century the Abbey d'Aulne had become a vast complex, the monks exploiting the local populace who worked for them under slave labour conditions while they filled their grain stores and accumulated wealth. No wonder when the French Revolution turned its attention to the monasteries there was enthusiastic help from the half-starved locals who joined the soldiers to torch and loot this abbey. Unfortunately along with the buildings many thousands of ancient books and rare manuscripts were also destroyed. In the grounds the abbey brewery had recently been resurrected and the following day we finished our wander around the majestic ruins with a glass or two of their produce, sitting outside surrounded by stunning scenery.

The river next took us to the medieval town of Thuin. On the way it led us past pretty villages and through rustic locks with collections of goats and chickens in the gardens alongside that stared inquisitively at this strange boat as we slowly came up into view. The approach to

Thuin is characterised by a succession of spits moored along the bank. They are all now long retired from service but kept spotless by the old bargees who continue to live on them. Decades before, Thuin had been known for its thriving boatyards but the sixties had brought a slow decline and now there were none left. The long line of barges was a tangible reminder of Thuin in its heyday.

We felt very welcome at the well kept town mooring with free electricity and water laid on for passing boaters and tied up behind a lovely wooden Dutch cruiser, the only other pleasure boat we had seen so far on this river. The owners of this immaculately kept craft lost no time to introduce themselves. Rose and Ronald had temporarily closed their café in the Netherlands and were here along with their elderly Labrador to spend August cruising in Belgium. They had brought more than a hundred bottles of champagne with them for the journey, some of which they generously shared with us that evening. While the two dogs enjoyed a swim together in the clear waters of the Sambre we asked Ronald if he knew why there were so few boats using this remarkably scenic waterway into France. The story he told was of another significant waterway route that had been allowed to close. It revealed the financial problems of maintaining a vast system and also touched on the tensions sometimes evident between France and Belgium. Allowed to become too silted to be useable, the Sambre just over the border had recently been closed to navigation, a state of affairs that was compounded by the dangerous state of two aqueducts also on the French side. There was talk of repairs and dredging with a possible re-opening in 2013 if funding could ever be agreed between the two countries. Keeping a look out for flying pigs, we amended our guide book and maps. We wondered how much longer this part of the Sambre would stay open now that it didn't go anywhere and was consequently hardly used, and decided to cruise on as near to the French border as we could after we had left Thuin.

That decision was delayed for three days while we enjoyed this interesting town. It was built on two levels. The lower level ran along the river edge and was full of pretty stone cottages lining narrow streets. This was where some of the retired bargees who had decided to go back to the land lived and the walls and gardens of their houses were decorated with mementoes from their working days. Anchors, boathooks and navigation lights were a common sight and many of these homes had a plaque hanging over the door carved with the name of their barge. We climbed the steep cobbled paths to the second, higher level of Thuin. Here the houses were larger and more sophisticated. Here too was the market square, town hall and belfry whose carillon was playing loudly. Knowing the view from the belfry would be well worth a further climb we went inside and accompanied by the increasing decibels, puffed our way up the many stone steps to the viewing platform at the top.

From the river valley the boater cannot see the extent of the thick forests covering the hills in this southern part of Belgium so the view over Thuin and beyond came as a surprise. We could clearly see the course of the Sambre as it snaked through the valley below fringed with the long line of barges that we had passed on our way. As we looked towards the horizon thickly forested hillsides stretching for miles and miles dominated the view. We were amazed that in this small and heavily populated country this vast amount of dense forest had been allowed to remain unexploited and from our high viewpoint we could see the thick tree canopy was pushing close to Thuin's borders as if reluctant to let even this pretty town infringe its ancient rights. It was all so very different from industrialised Flanders in the north.

View of Thuin from the belfry showing line of retired 'spits'.

On our way back down the belfry stairs we passed a balcony where we could stop and watch the carillon player. Eventually noticing he had an audience, we were enthusiastically invited to join him. Without interrupting his recital he indicated the narrow steps that led us down to the carillon. It stood on a rickety wooden platform with a sheer unprotected drop to the ground floor far below. Mindful of this we carefully squeezed ourselves into the small space either side of the carillonist as he finished the piece he was playing so expertly. Here in the gloom of the belfry we felt very privileged to be so close to the beautifully made carillon with its multitude of wires connecting the keyboard to the many rows of heavy bells hanging high in the belfry from a network of thick wooden beams. It had been in use for hundreds of years and amazingly I was invited to sit down and have a go. As I formed two fists to strike the keyboard with – it may sound brutal but that's the technique – I suddenly realised that all the wooden keys were identically shaped. With no clues as to which note was which, the random noise my fists produced must have shocked the people of Thuin as it rang out over the hill tops. With much enthusiasm the carillon player explained the workings and the history of the instrument then finished our unofficial guide with a complicated Bach Prelude in which his fists flew around the keys. He had made our belfry visit very special. Descending the steps to the ground floor with wide smiles on our faces, the lady in the ticket office asked if we'd enjoyed our visit. Wonderful, we replied, especially the views and the unexpected invite by the carillon player. Her face fell. How many more times, she groaned, would she have to remind him that it was too dangerous for the public, that they had no insurance cover for impromptu visits to the carillon floor. She stormed off up the stairs leaving us wishing we had kept quiet about the endearing enthusiasm of the delightful carillonist.

There was still time to explore some paths signposted around the town that led eventually to the evocatively named 'Hanging Gardens'. We viewed them from a hilltop opposite, admiring these terraced strips of land that had first been cultivated in medieval times. Now they tumbled down from the high walled, ancient houses of Thuin and were used as vineyards, the first we had seen in Belgium. It got us wondering why Belgium was not known for its wine and we asked Rose and Ronald that evening as we downed yet more of their wonderful bubbly. Apparently Napoleon had ordered all the vineyards in Belgium to be scrubbed out and they had never been replanted, the Belgians concentrating on beer and chocolate instead. That was okay by us.

Of course there was going to be a festival during our stay in Thuin, had Belgium ever let us down? The elderly lady who passed *Snail* every evening to walk her ancient, blind dog had stopped to tell us the news. We could take part tomorrow and her son would give us tickets. This was all we could understand from her fast flowing and quietly spoken French and with Rose not around to translate for us we were left wondering what tomorrow would bring. The previous evening fluent French and English speaking Rose had been a willing interpreter as this long-time resident of Thuin told us a little about herself. Both her and her husband had been employed all their working lives at the boatyards in Thuin. During the second World War her husband had been in the 'secret army' and had been captured and imprisoned, lucky to survive. They had had a long marriage but now she was widowed and cared for by her son who we would meet at the festival. The following day we stepped outside the boat wondering what sort of celebrations we would find. We could see large groups of people standing along the roadside near the moorings and hoping they were something to do with the festivities, made our way there too. We hadn't previously noticed the unused tramlines still set into the road leading into the High Street. We hadn't even noticed the overhead wires that threaded through the town. The long line of assorted trams from a by-gone age that had suddenly appeared overnight were now making good use of them and were attracting a lot of interest. Immaculate and gleaming, these vintage vehicles had been saved from dereliction and brought back to service by a group of enthusiastic volunteers, one of whom was the son of the old lady. It was not surprising that with our limited French we had been unable to understand her description of this unusual festival.

Standing proudly by their trams waiting for customers, the volunteer drivers and conductors in their smart uniforms sold tickets that enabled passengers to try all the different trams that would be run for the entire day from Thuin to the next village of Lobbes and back. We bought our ticket and chose for our first of many tram trips that day to ride in a beautifully restored deep blue and dark wood 1930's example from the fascinating line-up. Some of the trams dated back to the turn of the century when comfort was not a consideration. With their open sides and wooden benches they looked very primitive compared with their later, more luxurious neighbours. We were keen to try as many as possible and were grateful it was such a sunny and dry day. Our chosen tram was now full of passengers and the driver set off towards the busy town centre. Thuin hadn't seen trams for many years and in the meantime cars had of course taken precedence. Many of these had been parked along the roadside while their owners went to the shops. The roadside also happened to be where the tramlines ran. As a consequence our journey was punctuated by frequent stops accompanied by much impatient stomping on the floor pedal that sounded the tram's bell as the driver summoned astounded car owners from their shopping who patently couldn't believe their eyes. Thuin's traffic was often in good humoured chaos that day as tram after tram rattled its way through the town and up the steep hillside track to Lobbes. That evening we shared our experiences of the day with Rose and Ronald and they, generous souls, shared more champagne. We also got talking about our experiences so far with our boat which led to them explaining why we kept hearing references to cigars on the VHF radio. It was a not totally complementary nick-name in Belgium for an English narrowboat. Now at last we knew.

Boating friendships are by nature transient encounters and well understood by those who indulge in them. The possibility of perhaps meeting again somewhere, sometime, makes goodbyes easier. We were all aware of this as we parted the next day in opposite directions, hoping that Rose and Ronald's lovely cruiser could still get under the bridges now that its 'ballast' had been so severely depleted. Three locks and two pretty village stopovers later we reached the last Walloon lock on the Sambre before the French border near Erquelinnes. The lockkeeper looked surprised to see a boat in his lock and shuffled out of his office. We produced our pile of computer generated paperwork given to us back at Charleroi, explaining that we would return again within the hour once we had reached the border. This news did not go down well with the lockkeeper who could not see any reason to put us through when we couldn't go far the other side. Grudgingly he worked the lock for us and as we descended, the molluscs clamped to the walls squirted water at us, perhaps instructed to do so by the disgruntled locky. On our return having got as near to the border as we could we were handed a new pile of papers without a word before the over-worked lockkeeper trudged back to his office to press a few more buttons on the lock control panel.

We stopped overnight at the now deserted Thuin moorings before the next day retracing our way back to Charleroi and once again through Belgium's worst lock. Here we were held up for so long that it was too late in the day to escape Charleroi's untidy urban sprawl and we found ourselves forced to stop for the night in rather insalubrious surroundings. The contrast with the beautiful and serene Haute Sambre could not have been greater. Later that same evening a small Dutch registered barge moored up in front of us and the skipper who unexpectedly hailed from Scotland introduced himself. He had recently bought the boat in Holland and was now making his way back slowly to the UK to fit it out as a new floating home for himself. Feeling more secure now that we were no longer alone on the mooring we turned in for the night but it wasn't long before rowdy, drunken voices very close to the boat woke us up. Our brave terrier joined us on the bed, trembling with fear. The loud splash from the stern that we heard next was not one of the drunks falling in but the sound of our rope that had been untied from the mooring bollard being thrown into the canal. Skipper grabbed our powerful torch and raced outside to catch the culprit about to do the same with our front ropes too. With much laughter, the group ran off. For the first time in Belgium we got out mooring chains and padlocks from the locker to secure *Snail* and then tried to get back to sleep. Our Scottish neighbour had slept through it all.

Leaving aside the dearth of kingfishers, the wildlife on the river flourished as we gradually swapped the industrial landscape for rural again. Stopping for the night on a lock wall in the countryside before we reached the city of Namur, the dog and I wandered off along the towpath for a late evening walk. A rustle in the trees at ground level made us both stop to look and listen. I could just make out the shadowy shape of a hefty looking mammal but it crashed back into the woods before I got a really good sighting. Back at the boat as we sipped our drinks outside in the bow, I wondered if there were muntjac or, more excitingly wild boar in these parts. A couple walking past stopped to ask if we had seen their rottweiler that had run off. Mystery solved.

Our mooring at Namur.

We spent the following five days in the city of Namur. The mooring, tied to railings on a high wall, was uncomfortably close to passing commercial traffic but the gems to be found in this city made the discomfort totally bearable. First of these was the Saturday market with its colourful and extensive flower stalls and local produce although marred for us by its inclusion of live animals and birds for sale in their disgracefully cramped cages, many with no water. Then it was on to the city's museum with its well presented, mainly Roman artefacts much of which had been dug up from the river bed. Outside in front of the town hall a band in colourful, eccentric costume playing bizarrely shaped home made instruments had attracted a large and good humoured crowd. The 'music' was an acquired taste and we soon walked on to admire the buildings in the oldest part of the city.

Our Jones' waterways guide had mentioned the existence of another museum containing the work of a medieval goldsmith. It sounded very interesting and so we approached the Namur tourist office for directions but the staff there hadn't heard of it. With a bit of detective work we found the convent where it seemed this collection was housed but there was nothing to say that this really was the place. There was a small door set into a wall and tentatively we rang the bell. The grille in the old door slid open and a woman's voice asked brusquely what we wanted. Pretty sure now that we'd got the wrong place, we hesitantly asked to see the Hugo d'Oignies collection. The grille was promptly snapped shut and then to our surprise, we heard the lock being opened and the door swung open. We were led in silence into the convent where a smiling receptionist asked for our bags and coats. Beckoned to continue to follow, we walked in silence through quiet corridors until our escort stopped at a small table with two chairs where we were invited to sit down. She disappeared behind a door and we were left wondering what would happen next. Warmly smiling, a nun appeared and invited us in to a small room filled with display cases glittering with jewel encrusted gold artefacts. She asked us to write our names and addresses in a little notebook then handed us an audio guide each. The nun sat down in a corner of the room and left us to revel in this beautiful collection. Throughout the centuries at times of unrest and war the entire collection had always been hidden away. Because of this it had miraculously survived intact for us to marvel at. The convent had been given it all for safe keeping during the Second World War when they squirreled the treasure trove away apparently hidden in a sack, with evident success. After the war the nuns had been allowed to keep the collection and now rather perversely these priceless objects were on display to the public in a tiny room with an ordinary looking door and no obvious security apart from the nun escort and the difficulty in finding it in the first place.

In the 13th century Hugo d'Oignies had trained as a goldsmith before he followed his three brothers into a monastic order. Here he had all the time he needed to perfect the gold filigree techniques that he originated and that are still used today. Word spread outside the monastery of this gifted monk and the beautiful objects that he was creating and wealthy women began to donate their jewels to him in the hope of ensuring their place in heaven for doing so. Some of these dated back to the Romans and so were already antiques in Hugo's time. He utilised them in a rather random way to adorn his gorgeous golden masterpieces simply using whatever he had been given at the time. Left until last, having exhausted the senses with the beauty and incredible skill of his work, the audio guide directed us to a tiny framed picture on the wall by the doorway. It was a comical but inconspicuous pen and ink cartoon of a monk that was so fresh looking that we were sure it was modern. In fact it was a delightful little self-effacing drawing done by Hugo of himself. Hugo it seems also had a delightful sense of humour.

Back at the boat and we had noticed that it was attracting more than a little attention from the people of Namur who often pointed at our cartoon snails painted on the side panels. The city's water taxis with their pretty canopies waved a welcome as they passed and their customers too turned to look and laugh at poor *Snail*'s artwork. All was revealed when we discovered a shop selling nothing but snail inspired souvenirs and also spotted a delightful bronze sculpture of two snails in the market place. The snail is Namur's symbol and all to do with the people of Namur's reputation for slowly speaking. Buying a local beer with a snail logo to try later, we walked back to the boat. We were moored opposite Namur's citadel, a foreboding place set high on a hill the other side of the river, it had formed a spectacular backdrop to our stay. Fortified by the snail beer we decided that afternoon it was time to attempt the steep walk up to the top. With each twist in the path the remains of additions and developments in the fortifications of the citadel from previous centuries were visible. The history to be found here was almost palpable. Out of breath by the time we had climbed to the top, we paused to enjoy the panoramic view of the river now far below us. Reading the developing story provided on the information boards as we climbed, we learnt that Namur's citadel had last been used in WW2 by the occupying forces and that throughout its history this mighty fortress had in fact never been successful in keeping invaders out. This in spite of Namur's citizens keeping up-to-date with the latest in stronghold design over the hundreds of years it had existed. Their efforts had certainly made for an atmospheric walk. Making one last expedition to the shops to buy another LW radio before we left Namur to replace the one I had accidentally 'drowned' a few days ago in the river and whose speakers had never fully recovered we were back to being BBC receivable and now ready to leave this captivating city.

The delightful bronze snail sculpture in Namur.

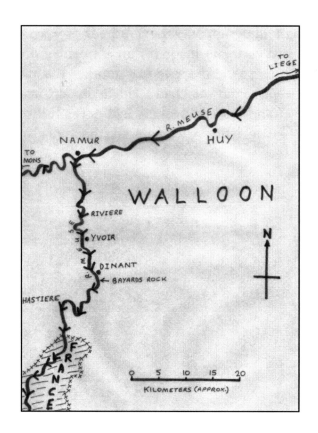

Hastiere to Huy.

CHAPTER 11.

The Meuse – where *Snail* finds herself lost in the locks.

Casting off on a busy commercial waterway can often be a fraught time. When mooring up we use four lines on *Snail* in an attempt to stop her jiggling around in the waves so much as the big stuff pushes past. When leaving, by the time we've undone three out of the four a 'commercial' will often appear, the sight of which causes an unseemly scramble to get another rope back on again FAST before *Snail* gets sucked irresistibly towards it. And it's not only amateur boaters who can get things wrong. As we were getting ready to leave Namur an almighty crash came from the river ahead. There trying to pass each other were two barges living up to their names by barging through the narrow 'T' junction formed at the meeting of the rivers Sambre and Meuse. Both had been taking the bends too fast and were now scraping along the walls and each other in an effort to extricate themselves, to the fascination of an embarrassingly large number of onlookers. As soon as the river ahead looked empty we took our chances, said 'au revoir' to Namur and turned right onto the mighty River Meuse at the junction.

After the intimacy and tranquillity of the Haute Sambre river, the majestic Meuse provided an immediate contrast. Wide and deep, we could feel *Snail* kick up her heels in enjoyment at the ease of movement that this broad waterway gave her. At this point the river is called the Haute (Upper) Meuse and leads eventually to France. It is a busy route for both commercial and pleasure craft and we soon saw why. For pleasure boaters it really is a stunning cruise in to France. The river has cut its way through a vast expanse of craggy rocks forming sheer, towering outcrops which are a climber's dream as well as a magnificent backdrop for boaters. For commercial vessels this unpredictable river has largely been tamed by the building of enormous hydraulic weirs next to the locks. These control the flood water making the river navigable all year round, in theory. In practice skippers told us of some scary experiences as they attempt to line up for a lock with flood water trying to pull their barge towards the weir instead and warned us not to try this ourselves. Mental note duly made to keep an eye on the weather forecast. Salmon also use this river and have not been forgotten by the barrage builders. To save them the struggle of attempting to jump the very high walls of the weirs they have their own route through a maze-like structure at each end. We never did see any fish trying to find their way through but were very impressed that their needs had been considered.

The towns and villages along this stretch of the Meuse have had to be built into the rock to have been built at all. Out of necessity roads hug the river banks and so do the houses, shops and occasional castle. Even the bigger towns are long and thin, the buildings grouped along either side of one main street. There is a distinctive architectural style in this region apparent on many of the older buildings that we passed. They featured attractive ornamental woodwork and acutely sloping rooflines often with the addition of little, pointy towers too small to be of any use, there just for visual impact.

Our first mooring was near the village of Riviere where we picked blackberries, Woody swam and a couple walked past on the rarely used towpath who stopped to tell us they had a narrowboat in Lichfield. It turned out to be a noisy stopover as we hadn't spotted the railway cut into the rock on the opposite bank. The twenty four hour freight trains that trundled along it made for a sleepless night. Rather drowsily we just managed a seven hour cruise the next day nearly to the French border. On the way if we peered hard at the vertical and precipitous rocks edging the river we could make out climbers hanging from brightly coloured ropes sometimes with buzzards circling above their heads in an interested way. The locks en route were busy. We shared the chambers with commercial traffic who refused to turn off their propellers and high revving trip boats who did the same, all of which constantly churned the water and kept us on our toes. The day trippers stared and stared and photographed our strange boat and its crew who seemed to be having so much trouble keeping control with their ropes.

We finally stopped for the night at the small town of Hastiere just before a high road bridge. It looked a peaceful spot with thankfully no sign of a railway. Two teenagers walked over to us. They were dressed only in shorts with towels tucked under their arms. They smiled shyly and instead of the usual questions about the boat, rather surprisingly asked if we knew how deep the river was. Well, no we didn't and while we puzzled over their question, they left their towels by the boat and ran off towards the bridge. By the time we had finished roping up, both boys were just visible looking over the edge of the bridge very high up above the river. After much hesitation, one boy clambered over the top and launched himself towards the water hitting it hard with a loud splash. We held our breath as we waited for him to re-appear. To our relief the boy bobbed up and waving happily to his friend to join him, he swam strongly to the bank. Sheepishly grinning and wrapped in their towels the two boys each accepted a 'pintje' (small, weak beer) and chatted pleasantly about their studies. Added to the many climbers we had seen dangling from the sheer rock faces, the youngsters in the Ardennes were certainly not risk adverse.

Hastiere had several attractions for us including dramatic stalactite filled caves and an ancient church still containing its twelfth century misericords. These rows of hinged and carved little wooden seats were provided for monks to rest their bottoms on during their extremely long services and made in such a way that it looks as though the user is still dutifully standing up. The beautifully executed wood carvings that we had come to see are hidden away under the seats where they can not be seen. This has helped to protect them through the passing of the centuries so that they are usually well preserved and because they are hidden, often comically vulgar. By the fifteenth century those at Hastiere were considered so rude even for the tastes of that time that many were 'censured' using a chisel to excise the offending part, a form of vandalism that we usually associated with the Victorians several centuries later. Outside the church there was a memorial plaque set into the wall. It recorded in harrowing detail the massacre of many of Hastiere's residents by the German occupying forces in WW1. So terrible were the events that when Hastiere was again occupied for a second time twenty years later, the Germans apparently trod more carefully.

It was now late in the afternoon and no sooner had we returned to *Snail* when one of the many trip boats on this river turned up and demanded to moor where we were. It was bigger than us, everything is, so late though it was we cast off and headed towards France. It turned out that the trip boat had done us a favour. As a consequence of our enforced move we found what was for us one of the best moorings in Belgium, just after the next lock. Peaceful and scenic, always a plus and on a low, narrowboat friendly wall, another plus point there was plenty of room even though one of the longest commercials we'd seen so far was already tied up. There was even free electricity. We stayed three days. Woody loved the complete freedom to swim and wander about. We all loved the long forest walks and being so close to the border might have crossed into France during one of them, who knows. Entertainment was unexpectedly provided by an unpowered go-kart race at the nearby village on the Sunday. Drivers of assorted ages sitting in an imaginative variety of home-made carts including a large armchair set on wheels were towed by a tractor up the winding hill that ran through the village and then let go. Straw bales lining the route cushioned the results of haphazard steering mechanisms and an amazing number made it all the way down again in one piece including the armchair.

On the fourth day we dragged ourselves away. It was now early September and we were mindful of the possibility of flood water that we had been warned about on this river. That scenario would become ever more likely as the summer turned to autumn so we felt we should push on. We were now heading back the way we had come, away from France and towards the town of Dinant. There were three locks to descend on the way and as we approached the second we became aware of a policeman stood by his car watching us from the bank. As we manoeuvred into the lock we could see that the policeman had driven ahead of us and had now got out of his car. He was peering down into the lock and was obviously waiting for us. This uncomfortable realisation was made all the worse by the crew of a Dutch cruiser already in the chamber who were watching our approach with fascination, presumably wondering what we had done. Which was what we were wondering too. As usual we need not have worried. The officer was fascinated by our boat and had simply stopped to ask us about it and to take pictures. The crew on the cruiser lost interest and looked away. The lock keeper leant out of his control tower and gave us a friendly wave before we all became preoccupied with our ropes as the water was gently let out of the chamber.

Dinant boasted a long row of very up-market town moorings with correspondingly up-market prices. There was room among the gin palaces and trip boats for *Snail* to squeeze in and raise the tone of the neighbourhood but we politely declined and instead pushed on rather a long way to a free wall on the far outskirts. A motorway bridge held aloft on tall pillars strode high across the river in front of us and disappeared over the hills on the other side. Towering right beside us was the legendary Bayard's Rock. This was a mooring steeped in history, folklore and intrigue. The oldest of the stories varies in the telling but centres around four thirteenth century knights and Bayard, their brave and loyal horse. It was while carrying the knights in a bid to escape their enemies that the horse struck the rock with his hoof, causing it to split away from the main cliff and leaving it set apart as it is today. A more recent tale tells the story of how the mountaineering Belgian monarch Albert the First climbed to the top of this sheer pinnacle and was pushed to his death by the jealous husband of his mistress. Historians maintain rather more mundanely that he was killed in an accident while climbing the rocks nearer to Namur. No-one disputes that the Rock witnessed scenes of fierce fighting in WW2 when the Allies pushed back the Germans during the Battle of the Bulge. It could have been an atmospheric place to stop but for the busy main road to Dinant running parallel to the wall above us. We tied up and began the long walk back into town.

Approaching Bayard's Rock to moor.

Dinant's fortified citadel is perched on a sheer cliff and reached via a white knuckle cable car ride, worth every heart stopping moment for the panoramic views of the river and town you get at the top. We hadn't realised when we bought our tickets that visitors who wanted to see the interior of the citadel would be forced to join an escorted group. We dutifully obeyed and tagged along with a small group of sightseers. With an English translation not on offer we were soon trying to unobtrusively creep away from the interminable and to us unintelligible ramblings of the guide. He was having none of it and spotting us getting away, grumpily ordered us back to the fold. After a further foiled escape attempt he kept an eagle eye on us and we never did discover anything about the history of Dinant's citadel but our visit to this ancient town did improve. The cathedral was lofty and beautiful and the café we chose to rest at before the long march back to the boat served the most wonderful advocaat smothered ice cream. It wasn't enough though to tempt us back the next day and instead we cast off towards Namur, stopping at the half way point that evening in a rural spot near Yvoir where the forest-covered hill behind us beckoned. A delightful climb through the trees followed and on reaching the top rewarded us with the well camouflaged, ivy clad ruins of a castle through which we could just make out *Snail* on the river far below us.

View from Dinant's citadel. We are moored near the bridge in the far distance.

Reaching Namur the next day we found that it was almost empty of pleasure boats even though it was still only the first week of September. That evening we looked at the maps to decide where to go next. The choice was to turn around and head back along the Sambre to our winter stopover at Lokeren via Charleroi again or hope for dry weather and risk a bit more Meuse. This would take us on the exciting and still new to us route through Antwerp. It wasn't such a difficult decision. The river from Namur was now known as the Moyen (Middle) Meuse. It is the watery highway to the industrial city of Liege and was consequently hectic with the 'big stuff' much in evidence. The locks on the Meuse towards Huy, the next sizeable town, were enormous. We shared the first of these locks with a commercial barge, two fully laden dumb (unmotorised) barges pushed by a tug and three large Dutch pleasure cruisers. The lockkeeper worked out that, quite incredibly to us, he still had room in his lock to shut off half the chamber to save time and water and we were therefore all beckoned to the front. While we descended, Skipper calculated that these mighty locks could accommodate ninety nine full length (70foot) narrowboats all at once.

Reaching Huy we shunned the moorings at the two yacht clubs in favour of a high, rather unsuitable wall very close to the town. This way we kept hold of the twenty one euros a night the yachties would have charged us but did have to put up with the constant pull on our ropes of the closely passing river traffic as it rushed by day and night. The howling gale didn't help either, c'est la vie. We must have become immune to the discomfort as my diary records a three day stop here. We were joined briefly on our wall by Dutch cruisers who came and went and warned by a trip boat on day two to untie our ropes from the railings before the police saw us and fined us five hundred euros. We huffed and puffed up the hill to Huy's citadel – the gale was still blowing so the cable car wasn't running – and learned about its very grim and barbarous history in the last two wars when it was used as a prison. We endured the cracked bells of Huy's carillon that attempted to play Ode to Joy every hour and we discovered the old part of town where we also found Huy's police station and courts. They were housed in ancient buildings that had been a refuge centuries before for the displaced monks of the ransacked Abbey d'Aulne on the Sambre. With that unexpected connection linking our travels over the past weeks on these two lovely Ardennes rivers, we were ready to head for Liege and the end of the Meuse.

Moored at Huy, view from the citadel.

Medieval fountain in Huy's marketplace.

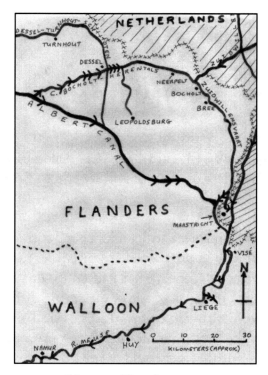

Liege to Turnhout.

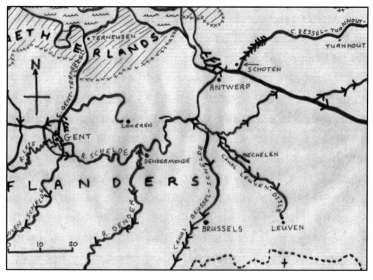

Turnhout to Lokeren.

CHAPTER 12.

Albert Canal to Lokeren – in which *Snail* becomes attached, Skipper finds live reminders of the past and we add to Belgium's cuisine.

It was now the second week in September and fortunately the weather was still on our side as we moved towards Liege and the end of the Meuse. The majestic scenery that had continued to accompany us suddenly changed to miles of active quarrying disfiguring the rocky cliffs. These were now alive with dust covered site lorries moving around busily like ants on a mound. It began to prepare us for the industrial landscape that we would see on both sides of the river when we reached Liege. At the last lock on the Meuse just on the outskirts of the city we were called in by the lock keeper to share with a two thousand ton commercial. We tied up to the bollards on the chamber wall and waited to descend. The empty barge next to us was towering above us but we were well used to this by now and calmly changed the ropes to lower and lower positions as the water emptied from the lock. The chamber gates swung open and as usual from my position in the front of the boat I looked behind to Skipper at the back to wait for him to nod. This was my instruction to let go of the front rope from the bollard so that we could leave the lock chamber. I was sure that I saw him nod although he always insists that he didn't and just at the moment that I let my rope go, the empty commercial next to us inexplicably (and unnecessarily) put on full power and began to plough past us. The inevitable happened, *Snail* was irresistibly sucked towards the barge as if by a magnet and with a nasty thud she stuck fast to its pristine blue paintwork. For a few terrifying moments we were pulled along with the ship before the barge skipper saw what had happened and reduced his speed. A crew member came over to look down at us still clamped to his barge and complained bitterly about his paintwork. What about ours, I replied angrily and still shaking with fright watched as our portside bow thruster finally managed to push us free. The commercial exited at a more sensible speed and we mulled over how near to disaster we had come. From that time on we had a new golden rule to add to the ones that with growing experience we had already formulated to cope more safely with these very different waterways. We would never in future remove our ropes in a lock until all the commercial traffic had left it.

Postponing a visit to Liege with its high rise tower blocks for another time we pushed on, leaving the Meuse and entering the Albert Canal. Jones describes this as a motorway of a canal, one of the widest, deepest and busiest in Belgium. Taking eight years to dig, it was finished in 1939 then widened even more in the 1960's. The locks can take ships of 12,000 tons. Poor little *Snail*, she really would be with the 'big stuff' now. We were getting desperate to fill our water tank and having satisfied ourselves that *Snail* could handle the choppy waves that the passing shipping produced (record size of vessel that had overtaken us so far was 4,200tons) turned off the canal at the Darse Vise. A 'darse' is a commercial dock arm and normally not suitable for us but this one was in a rural setting and evidently hadn't been used industrially for some time. The lady skipper on the peniche moored in front of us came over to lend a hand. She told us that she was now retired but her family still ran a very successful training school for would-be commercial skippers in Huy if we felt like giving it a go. Relaxing outside that evening we were joined by gangs of little owls in the trees lining the bank and noctule bats swooping around the boat making we hoped good inroads into the numbers of mosquitoes that were also making their presence felt. Every so often that night while lying safely under our mosquito net we would be reminded by the rocking of the boat that commercial activity on the Albert was only a little way away. Joining that again could wait until the morning when we really did have to find water.

Next day and a few kilometres further up the Albert Canal we reached the confluence with the Canal de Lanaye and three land borders to choose from. We were still in Walloon, just. If we took the Lanaye on our right we would enter the Netherlands heading for Maastricht. If we continued north on the Albert we would be in

Flanders albeit still skirting the outskirts of that aforementioned famous Dutch city. Choices, choices. We chose the latter and ploughed on a little further through very choppy waters to the junction with the Zuidwillemsvaart canal where we decided to turn off and continue our now very desperate search for water. We knew from our old maps that the second of the two deep locks at the start of this pleasant canal had a tap somewhere. They are normally situated inside the locks but not this one. Once through the lock we pulled over and tried to find it. The lock keeper was unusually unhelpful for a Flemming or perhaps we hadn't understood his meagre directions but eventually we discovered the tap well camouflaged and totally hidden under a small brick built cover. We connected our hosepipe and then waited and waited as the tap reluctantly drip fed our empty tank. It was even slower than the infamous British Waterway's canalside taps. With at last a full tank but now rather late in the day we stopped a little further on at the village of Rekem, *Snail* causing the usual stir with the locals. The Zuidwillemsvaart continues through Belgium into the Netherlands and this was a village with a Dutch feel to it already. Pretty in a well manicured and orderly kind of way with some old and expensive looking properties for us to admire, we were definitely not in Walloon now.

It was a peaceful cruise to the town of Bree the next day. This straight and largely rural canal can only cope with smaller commercials and we enjoyed the 'calm' after the 'storm' of the Albert. Anne and Hendrik had arranged for us to meet a friend of theirs here. His name was Brecht and he ran a very well known coffee shop (but not of the Dutch variety!). The shop was delightfully old fashioned and aromatic and we were given the usual generous Belgian welcome but first we were asked to turn off our mobile phone. Along with computers and other electronic gadgetry they were not allowed in his shop. I looked over to the elaborately decorated and manually operated till and was transported immediately back to the 1950's but then the entire shop looked as if it had remained in that decade. Brecht asked us in depth how we liked our coffee and selected some beans from one of the many bulging Hessian sacks strewn around the shop. He then roasted them to the point that he thought we would enjoy from our description and popped them in a bag. He then repeated this with some beans from another sack and another until we had several little bags to take back with us and enjoy. The smell from all this roasting of beans for us coffee lovers was just heavenly. The least we could do that evening was to show Brecht around the boat and share a few beers. When he asked if he could find us again the following day and bring two friends along we looked forward to it although had to point out that, as usual, we didn't know where that would be.

A few kilometres from Bree the canal branches off to the right and soon crosses the border to the Netherlands. We again chose to stay in Belgium and took the left branch, the bosky Bocholt-Herentals Canal. Our Jones guidebook implied that inviting sounding moorings would be no problem on this quiet waterway but as was so often the case we found they were only suitable for cruiser length (and height) boats. We tried at three different spots but either the finger pontoons provided were too short or they were at our gunwale height which was too dangerous if a passing commercial swept us under them. Finally we found a suitable spot along the canal bank at the town of Neerpelt and immediately attracted spectators from the nearby campervan park and yacht haven. It wasn't too far by car for Brecht and his friends to also find us and we had another very pleasant and interesting evening facilitated as ever by the local brewery's products.

Two days later we braved the drizzle to cruise another ten kilometres and found an ideal mooring surrounded by pine forests at the junction with a dead-end canal, the Beverlo. Woody took advantage of the safe freedom here to dash about among the trees while the red squirrels that abounded in these forests got smartly out of his way high up in the canopy. Many of the trees had posters attached to them with graphic pictures warning walkers about a type of caterpillar that was swarming that year, infesting the pines and causing a nasty rash if touched. We kept a watch out for them but never did see one, let alone a swarm. Perhaps by mid September they had moved on. Walking back to the boat we stopped to look at a very rusty spits moored a little way from *Snail*. It looked as if no-one had used it for many years and was in a rather squalid state so we were surprised to see the back cabin door open and an elderly lady in a flowery wrap-over dress emerge. She was carrying a bucket and walked behind the cabin to the stern where she dipped the bucket over the side. To save her and our embarrassment we turned away back to *Snail* as still standing outside, she began to wash in the canal water she had collected for the purpose.

The next day was a Sunday, cold but sunny. The Beverlo beckoned and with no locks to contend with we thought we would cruise to the end of the canal at the town of Leopoldsburg (named after the king who had put up the money) and then come back again to the junction, a distance of about thirty kilometres and easily do-able in a day. We cruised along forest lined banks through crystal clear water not passing another boat until we got nearer to Leopoldsburg when a small cruiser went by full of people smiling and waving to us. "They've got a lot of friends." we said. And then another went past, even more full than the first and then another. They looked dangerously overloaded for such small boats and we were now very puzzled. Soon we saw that the grassy banks leading to the town were teaming with people enjoying the colourful craft and beer stalls that had been erected along the edge of the canal. They shouted a welcome to us as we cruised through to the turning basin at the head of navigation. This we found to be chock-a-block with vintage boats from wooden cruisers to heavy tugs and just as we were wondering how on earth we would find room to turn around the crew on one of the tugs invited us to stop alongside them and join in. We had stumbled upon another wonderful Belgian festival and the cruisers we had seen were giving unofficial boat trips to the people of Leopoldsburg. The following day we said goodbye to our new friends and with only a slight hangover slowly made our way back along the Beverlo at the very sedate speed of 2knots, stuck behind a well loaded spits who had to keep to the centre of the narrow channel where it was deepest. That was okay, we were definitely in no rush.

The town of Turnhout was our next destination which we reached after six hours (a long day for us) on the snappily named Kanaal van Dessel over Turnhout naar Schoten. This is one of four canals built by the government in the 1800's to promote the economy in the poor region of Kempen and we had now travelled on three of them. They were all rural and peaceful with only small pockets of industry every so often. Many of the lock sides were adorned with specimen trees that added a certain grace to the scenery until we descended in the deep locks at which point they disappeared. Limited commercially to

600tons, while we were there at the end of the summer little else was moving on these now under-used waterways and the only drawback for us was the dearth of suitable and free moorings. The good people of Leopoldsburg had already been in touch with the harbour master at Turnhout's yacht haven to expect an English 'cigar'. Through their kind intervention we were given a substantial discount on the usual mooring fee for our long boat and subsequently spent two days there. Turnhout reminded us of Gainsborough in England as both towns have ancient buildings that can surprise the unwary visitor because of their incongruous setting. Gainsborough has a beautiful medieval manor house that was saved from its proposed destruction to make way for a car park by the public outcry at this civic vandalism. It now stands marooned in a sea of modern shops and apartments. Turnhout has a twelfth century castle built in the local and lovely red brick and still with its moat. It too is almost totally surrounded by new shops and offices although the width of the moat has to a certain extent helped to keep this less refined neighbourhood at bay. After falling into neglect in the last century it is now used as a law court and looked sparklingly pristine when we were there.

Turnhout Castle.

Turnhout had many more notable and off-beat places of interest to discover. It had the last remaining water tower in Belgium and this was bizarrely situated in the middle of one of the town's streets. It had been covered in modern art work in a style that we were beginning to recognise as unique to Belgium. Following in a centuries – old tradition of paper making Turnhout boasted a flourishing factory devoted to making playing cards which were exported all over the world. The museum attached to the factory was fascinating and on returning to the boat discovered we too had a pack of cards brought with us from Norfolk that had been made in Turnhout. The serenely beautiful Turnhout Beguinage was as beautifully kept as its equivalent in Kortrijk and our visit there should have been a relaxing end to the day until Skipper made a find when walking the dog that evening. Sticking up out of the towpath beside the canal he could see what looked like rounds of live ammunition. Carefully extricating it from the earth it turned out to be an entire beltful of the stuff. A passing dog walker didn't look at all surprised at his find suggesting he left it at the side of the path and she would tell the police. The next day this evocative reminder of Belgium's past had gone and her nonchalance was easily explained when we learnt a few more facts. Every year Belgian farmers unearth WW1 ordnance when ploughing their fields. In spite of using armour plating on their tractors, every year farmers die. Every year a specialist army team put together for the purpose picks up and makes safe more than 200tons of live ammunition and chemical weaponry that are uncovered mainly by farmers who put their finds in heaps by the sides of fields and roads ready for collection. Every year the remains of around thirty bodies killed in WW1 are also recovered. The army estimates that there are probably 450 million live pieces of ordnance still to be found so they will be kept busy with their dangerous work for a while longer yet.

The many lift bridges on these canals had been operated for us extremely efficiently up to now by teams of keepers in their vans. So much so that we had taken for granted that they would magically rise up at our approach and so expertly timed that we didn't have to slow down, consequently not holding up the road traffic for longer than was necessary. Leaving Turnhout and reaching the next lift bridge we realised this was about to change when it remained resolutely down. A passer-by saw us, turned around and walked briskly back to a roadside café. Several minutes later the disgruntled keeper emerged and eventually the bridge went up. At the next after several sounds of *Snail*'s horn, a sleepy and dishevelled keeper emerged from his office and was just about roused to do his job. The next promised to be easier as we could see the keeper feeding his livestock by the bridge. He saw us too but continued to lovingly tend to his assorted flocks rather than us. Oh well, we weren't in a rush.

Unusual lift bridge on the way from Turnhout.

Suitable free moorings were like hen's teeth on this canal and so it was with much difficulty that we finally found somewhere to stop for the night after doing three of the last nine locks that would lead to the small town of Schoten and the end of this canal system. We had spent the evening before at Turnhout yacht haven chatting with another English boater on his tjalk (a type of Dutch boat with sweeping curves) over a few beers and too many friets. He had jokingly suggested making a soup with the leftovers so that evening I gave his idea a try.

Belgian friet (or British chip) soup:
Chop up two onions and a stick or two of celery. Put into a large, heavy based saucepan and fry gently til soft in a little olive oil.
Cut up the leftover friet into smaller pieces and add. Stir around then add enough vegetable or chicken stock to amply cover. Bring to the boil, cover and simmer for 5 minutes or until celery tender.
Whizz til smooth, add a little salt and loads of pepper to taste and serve with a swish of cream or crème fraiche.

Schoten lies at the junction with the Albert Canal which for us this time would lead to Antwerp, the tidal River Scheldt and ultimately, Lokeren. We tied up at Schoten's yacht harbour as there was nowhere else, paid our dues and hoped for a good night's sleep before a very long day. Late in the evening an English flagged cruiser tied up in front of us although the owners turned out to be Irish and Welsh. This explained the Gaelic-sounding name prominently displayed on the stern of their boat which with a grin they translated for us. It meant 'kiss my arse', an invitation to the grumpy French lockkeepers that they had come across on their travels. Next day we both shared the last two locks before the junction with the Albert Canal hoping in each that the lockkeeper's Gaelic vocabulary was poor. An upset locky is not good news when you are so dependant on them. At the junction we went our separate ways and so began a shattering non-stop nine hour day that took us first through the busy port of Antwerp, from there to face five hours on the choppy and tidal River Scheldt eventually turning off towards the peaceful River Dender at Dendermonde lock. What a welcome sight that was as it meant only another hour to go before we could moor up at Denderbelle, the next lock along the river where we knew we would get a quiet night's sleep and Woody could finally uncross his legs. We so admired the two British couples on their commercial barges that we had met in Gent all those months before who regularly put in twelve hour days to be on time with their loads. Wimps that we were the next day was spent recovering and relaxing in the sunshine before a very early morning start to catch the tide on the Scheldt again, this time heading for Gent and our last few days before we stopped for the winter.

Moored at Denderbelle Lock.

It was good to be back at Tolhuis on the outskirts of Gent where we had first met Anne and Hendrik on their boat and then Rik and Nelly several months before. Needing water we stopped in the lock before mooring up. For once there were other boats and barges needing to go through so while we waited for our tank to slowly fill we went up and down and up again in the lock chamber with them. As soon as we had finished, left the lock and tied up, Rik spotted us. He wandered over and with a broad, welcoming smile asked how long were we staying. Four days later we had spent many happy times in their company, exploring more of historic Gent with its inviting cafés and helping where we could with the last stages in the fitting out of their yacht. It was during this time with them that we learnt of Rik's colourful past careers which included filling the pralines in a chocolatier's shop, racing motorbikes, owning a horse farm and becoming a famous postman. Rik told us that he often used to ride one of his horses into Gent where he tied it up to a tree outside a café while he had a beer or three. His riding talents came into national renown when while a postman he won a contest set by the post office to travel Belgium on horseback. This was to be part of the celebrations commemorating the post office's five hundred year anniversary and Rik's antics as he travelled were widely and popularly reported on Belgian television.

Sadly it was time to leave the stimulating company of our friends for the last leg of the journey back to Lokeren and our rather long 'winter' break that neither of us was really looking forward to. We had taken to this water gypsy lifestyle and found it difficult to cope with the thought of months of staying put. With many of the smaller waterways in Belgium closed until the spring we would have had to mainly cruise on the commercial ones. Feeling that this would in the end have become too monotonous the decision was made to stop.

Alongside Wim's boat for the winter. Note the crowd of cruisers at the town end.

That last day for us on the Moervaart to Lokeren happened to also be the last day of official pleasure boating in Belgium for that year and we were unexpectedly accompanied through the lift bridges by twelve cruisers from the local boat club making the most of it. After we had all gone through the last of the seven bridges the cruisers put their collective feet down and made a dash for it thinking no doubt that we would take up too much of the visitor mooring in Lokeren so just had to get there first. As we pulled up alongside Wim's boat we could see them crowded on the pontoon in the distance near the town and felt naughtily smug with ourselves. Wim came out to greet us and help us get comfortably settled in. His lovely historic boat towered above us and we felt completely at home.

Lightning Source UK Ltd.
Milton Keynes UK
UKOW03f0903080913

216743UK00001B/13/P